The French
and Indian War

BOOKS BY COLONEL RED REEDER

THE FRENCH AND INDIAN WAR
HEROES & LEADERS OF WEST POINT
WEST POINT PLEBE
WEST POINT YEARLING
WEST POINT SECOND CLASSMAN
WEST POINT FIRST CLASSMAN
SECOND LIEUTENANT CLINT LANE: WEST POINT TO BERLIN
CLINT LANE IN KOREA
ATTACK AT FORT LOOKOUT
WHISPERING WIND
THE SHERIFF OF HAT CREEK
THE MACKENZIE RAID
THE STORY OF THE CIVIL WAR
THE STORY OF THE REVOLUTIONARY WAR
THE STORY OF THE WAR OF 1812
THE STORY OF THE SPANISH-AMERICAN WAR
THE STORY OF THE MEXICAN WAR
THE STORY OF THE SECOND WORLD WAR, VOLS. 1 AND 2
SHERIDAN: THE GENERAL WHO WASN'T AFRAID
TO TAKE A CHANCE
THE STORY OF THE FIRST WORLD WAR
THE NORTHERN GENERALS
THE SOUTHERN GENERALS
ULYSSES S. GRANT
MEDAL OF HONOR HEROES
POINTERS ON ATHLETICS
THREE PITCHERS: ON THE MOUND
BORN AT REVEILLE
ARMY BRAT
DWIGHT D. EISENHOWER: FIGHTER FOR PEACE
OMAR N. BRADLEY: THE SOLDIERS' GENERAL

With NARDI REEDER CAMPION

THE WEST POINT STORY
BRINGING UP THE BRASS

THE FRENCH
AND INDIAN WAR

by
COLONEL RED REEDER

Maps by
Edward J. Krasnoborski

THOMAS NELSON INC.
Nashville / New York

First edition

Library of Congress Catalog Card Number: 76-181680

International Standard Book Number: 0-8407-6208-9
0-8407-6209-7

Manufactured in the United States of America

Photo of Robert Rogers reprinted from *Robert Rogers of the Rangers*, by John R. Cuneo. Copyright © 1959 by Oxford University Press, Inc. Reprinted by permission.

For
RUSSELL PHILIP REEDER

CONTENTS

LIST OF MAPS

9

AUTHOR'S NOTE

This story is about the French and Indian War of 1754–1763. Descriptions of some of the earlier combat in America is included to show the horrors of Indian border warfare and to tell of previous struggles in the area.

The French and Indian War was a fight for North America. Although Europeans viewed the conflict as an unimportant sideshow to the war on their continent, it was of tremendous concern to Americans and Canadians. Many Indian tribes became involved, but their viewpoints were limited and confused; they were anxious to be on the winning side, and in the end they lost.

Details in this war for possession of the North American continent have been overshadowed by events of the American Revolution. The war of 1754–1763 was as vital to our destiny as our fight for independence in 1775–1783.

The French and Indian War was marked by tremendous expenditure of effort, great problems of time and distance, and by fights on rough terrain. In addition, there were poor direction and control. The generalship varied from miserable depths to brilliant heights. The British and their colonials, as well as the French and the Canadians, frequently paid penalties when politics, jealousies, and greed for personal profit interfered with supply of soldiers in the wilderness and with the planning of campaigns.

In describing this story, which has greatly intrigued me, I received extraordinary help and guidance from a professional military historian of top rank, Colonel John R. Elting, United States Army, retired, of Cornwall-on-Hudson, New York. He not only reviewed the manuscript, but in places he added to it. His grasp of numerous aspects of the war, as well as his knowledge of Indian tribes, was extremely beneficial.

I am also indebted for the invaluable, painstaking, and efficient work of my editor-at-home, my wife, Dort Darrah Reeder. She typed the manuscript several times, as she did other manuscripts in this story-of-the-war series. She also questioned parts of this work that needed shoring and prepared the index.

I am grateful, too, for the help of Mr. Egon Weiss, adroit and unusual librarian, United States Military Academy, West Point, New York, and for work pertaining to research by members of his staff, principally Miss Nancy Harlow, Miss Charlotte Snyder, Miss Irene Feith, Mrs. Marie T. Capps, Mr. Edward Rich, Mr. Kenneth Rapp, Mr. Alan Aimone, Mrs. Jennie Ruth Murphy, and Mr. Stanley Tozeski.

General Bruce C. Clarke, Mr. Mert Akers, Colonel Pat Dionne, Colonel T. F. Plummer, and Mr. Nelson De Lanoy gave me assistance, as did Mr. William L. McDowell, Jr., deputy director of the South Carolina Department of Archives and History. I also am grateful to Major William L. Mills, Jr., of Concord, North Carolina, for his work. I thank Mr. Richard T. Wood, manager of Book Programs, University Microfilms, Ann Arbor, Michigan, for permissions pertaining to the trials of the Reverend John Williams, as related in the original writing: *The Redeemed Captive Returning to Zion*, University Microfilms' series *March of America*.

RED REEDER

Garrison, New York

The French
and Indian War

CHAPTER I

TOMAHAWKS AGAINST THE DOOR

Deerfield, Massachusetts, February 29, 1704

WHEN the Reverend John Williams heard war whoops, he sprang from his bed. The noise at his door sounded as if a drummer had gone mad. Windows crashed in his front room. The glow from logs in the fireplace highlighted red streaks on the faces of the Indians climbing in. The shocking scene and the noise did not stop John Williams. He ran to awaken two Massachusetts soldiers sleeping in the house, then dashed to his bedside for his pistol.

The front door crashed open and about twenty Indians charged in. Williams aimed at the leader. His pistol misfired. He said later this saved his life. Three Indians seized him and held their hatchets over his head. Abnaki Indians carried two screaming Williams children out into the snow. A Caughnawaga brave wrestled the maid outside. Suddenly, the children's cries of "Father!" stopped. Williams could guess why.

The Indians ripped off Parson Williams' clothes and bound him hand and foot. Two of them staggered downstairs, dragging Mrs. Williams. They threw her on the hearth. A procession of savages trooped out, their arms laden with blankets, cooking utensils, and clothing. Williams prayed out loud.

One of the soldiers, on duty in Deerfield, Massachusetts, and stationed in the house, jumped out of a bedroom window and escaped. This was Private John Stoddard. Fortunately, he had grabbed a cloak. Stoddard ran for help, out of Deerfield, down the snowy trail toward the next Massachusetts town of Hatfield, ten miles away. After a few hundred yards he stopped to rip the cloak into bindings for his feet. The actions of the other soldier stationed in Williams' house have not been recorded by history.

Shots rattled in the night. About seventeen Massachusetts soldiers who were stationed in the town tried to battle the raiders. According to the accounts, the attacking French and Indians varied in number from 200 to 340. The handful of militia withdrew before this overpowering force.

An hour later, the Indians ran back into the Williams home and dragged the minister and his wife out into the snow. A French officer, bundled up in furs and buckskin and looking almost like one of the Indians except for the sword at his belt and a bright gorget (throat armor) at his neck, inspected the house. Minutes later, the Indians set it afire. Other Deerfield homes went up, the red flames reflecting on the snow. Smoke billowed from the Williams' barn.

When dawn broke, Major Hertel de Rouville, French leader of the raiders, and his three brothers, inspected the captives—over one hundred sorry-looking men, women, and children. The major shouted at them, "You will keep up on the march! If you don't—" He made a downward slash with his sword. "Three hundred miles to Canada," he finished.

Under a bright blue sky, with sunlight dancing on the snow, the captives and their guards started north, the prisoners burdened with plunder. Plodding along with their parents were five surviving Williams children. The date was February 29, 1704.

The column passed snowshoe prints on a high drift at the stockade that indicated how the French and Indians had entered Deerfield. The attackers had spent the bitter night hidden in the forest two miles away; Major Hertel had allowed no fires. The Massachusetts soldiers on guard were not as well disciplined. Just before the raiders ran over the stockade, the sentries had forsaken their posts for the warmth of Deerfield homes. There is a story that before the guards moved inside they built snowmen to take their places at the gate.

Black ruins of the town, some of them still smoldering, matched the prisoners' hopes. But somehow the ornate door of the Williams home survived. It was as staunch as Parson Williams' faith.

The column wound its way up the Connecticut River, under no pressure to hurry. Major Hertel did not know that Private Stoddard had gone for help, but Hertel had a strong rear guard ready to ambush any that might arrive.

Assistance for the prisoners never appeared. When the column of captives and guards halted to adjust packs, Hertel spoke to Parson Williams. "Our losses were three brave French soldiers and eight Indians, five of them Maquas [Dutch for Mohawks]. Deerfield lost forty-nine."

It was hiking of the hardest kind, through deep March snows, over the frozen Green Mountains. John Williams supported his wife Eunice as best he could, but each day her strength ebbed. A few weeks before she had given birth to a child. At the Green River a chief barked at him, "Tell her good-bye. You go!"

Not long after Williams forded the river, he was told that his wife had stumbled in the water and that an Indian had smashed her skull with his tomahawk. It took every ounce of courage Parson Williams and his children had to keep walking. Indians carried the smallest Deerfield children, but they killed a "sucking infant" and a girl of eleven, and cut off the head of a Massachusetts soldier who could not keep up. On the fourth day, another lagging captive was killed by a tomahawk.

There was a lot of iron and Moses in John Williams. In spite of the tragedies he set the example, trudging on and on, his children at his side. Behind walked his people. They were also his children.

The deep snow made the minister's legs ache, and he limped badly. When Major Hertel ordered a brief camp, the Indians killed five moose for food and made Williams a pair of snowshoes from the hides.

On a Sunday, Hertel permitted Williams to preach. The captives huddled around fires as the minister chose for his text the eighteenth verse of the first chapter of Lamentations: "The Lord is righteous; for I have rebelled against his commandment: hear, I pray you, all people, and behold my sorrow: my virgins and my young men are gone into captivity." Early the next morning, the column toiled over the frozen landscape farther and farther away from New England.

The loss of the people of Deerfield shook the frontier. The devastated town lay but sixty miles from Albany, New York, and only seventy-five from Boston. Northern settlers howled for soldiers and militia to protect them. Citizens of other towns wondered when they would be struck. There seemed to be no protection from savagery sweeping in from the north.

CHAPTER 2

INTENSE HATRED

WHILE near panic rattled frontier settlements, the more than one hundred exhausted Deerfield captives hiked into the town of Chambly, near Montreal. It was the twenty-fifth day of their march. On each day a Deerfield prisoner had died.

The French townspeople treated the captives kindly. Williams was placed in a feather bed. But when church bells tolled, summoning citizens to Mass, Williams' Congregationalist faith suffered an even greater trial than it had undergone at the murder of his wife and two children. He refused to go to church. Frenchmen and Jesuit fathers wrestled him toward it. The Jesuits, furious over his obstinacy, appealed every way they could, but converting Parson Williams was like converting a rock.

The fearless Jesuits, who carried Christianity to the wild

Indian tribes and who worked to help them, possessed faith as firm as Williams' own. No one had greater belief than Father Jogues and the other Jesuit martyrs who had suffered mutilation and death at the hands of the savages. The torture the Jesuits received, much of it at the hands of the Iroquois, was fiendish. Christian Hurons described the persecution of Jesuit Fathers Jean de Brébeuf and Gabriel L'Alemant:

> The Iroquois tied them naked to posts . . . made six hatchets red hot [stringing some of them together] placing some about the necks, applying some of the hatchets to their loins and armpits.

Jesuits and British and French colonists suffered. Border warfare blazed on an irregular line. Settlers in Maine believed Jesuit Sebastien Râle, spiritual director of the Abnakis, had incited this tribe to raid settlements.

Just as aggressive as Râle was the egotistical missionary Abbé Le Loutre. In the minds of these two Jesuits, and some Protestants, border fighting was religious war. The conduct of the two Jesuits was far removed from the principles of the sixteenth-century founder of the order, Saint Ignatius Loyola.

The Jesuits in the Canadian town could not make Parson Williams abandon his religion, but they did convert his daughter Eunice, who eventually married a Caughnawaga, a Canadian "Praying Indian."

After a year of captivity, John Williams and fifty-seven of his fellow citizens returned to Boston by ship, redeemed through the help of the French governor of Canada, Philippe de Vaudreuil, although he had approved of the raid against Deerfield. Massachusetts looked like the Promised Land to the long-suffering survivors.

Bloody raids, with scalped bodies, burning cabins, and strings of captives hiking to Canada had occurred long before the French and Indians smashed Deerfield in 1704. Raids were the hallmark of border clashes along the undefined line between French and British colonies.

It was not always the French and Indians who were the aggressors. In 1689, a war party of fifteen hundred Iroquois paddled canoes in a hailstorm across a lake near Montreal to crash into the town of Lachine, staging one of the bloodiest and most fearsome butcheries in the history of Canada. Actually, after first reports were sifted, it turned out that not all of Lachine was wiped out, but the Iroquois had killed two hundred French, roasted and eaten five children, burned fifty-six of seventy-seven houses, and taken ninety prisoners.

After the vicious Lachine raid, Count Frontenac, a cruel and experienced soldier, again became governor of Canada. He sent exaggerated reports of the Lachine horror to his king, Louis XIV. Frontenac's mind burned with hatred of the Indians. He was motivated not only by desire to revenge the Lachine raid, but by ambition. Actually he accomplished little except to keep the fires of war going.

Like many leaders, Frontenac had a streak of the actor in him. He dazzled Canadian Indians by appearing in a wide-brimmed and plume-decked hat and bright silks with a rapier hanging from his belt. Later, he daubed red and blue paint on his face and, although he was sixty-nine years old, danced and howled with his warriors around council fires. He wrapped himself in a cloak of revenge, telling his Indian allies, "I will lead you on raids so fierce our enemies will crave peace."

Frontenac inspired Canadian Indians. When he could not keep up on the raids he originated, his men carried him in a chair. When they traveled by water, they lifted him over rough portage trails in his canoe. In the next eight years, he inspired raids against Schenectady, New York, Salmon Falls, New Hampshire, and Falmouth, Maine. He also sent the Abnakis crashing into Wells, Maine, Durham, New York, and Haverhill, Massachusetts. This hard-

"Two Ottawa Chiefs, Vicinity of Lake Huron." Watercolor by Sir Joshua Jebb.

Courtesy Peabody Museum, Harvard University

working leader also bred bitter hatred in Canada, and on his warpaths he took time to wipe out hundreds of Iroquois along the Mohawk in New York.

Hatred was also bitter on the New England side of the border. Men who had seen the results of Frontenac's raids, and who had lost friends and families, thirsted for revenge. New Englanders were farmers or fishermen, sometimes both. None were skilled woodsmen and hunters like the French Canadians who led Indian raids, but the New Englanders did know ships and hard work. And a few were slowly learning about the woods. When they became proficient in living and fighting in the forests, the French and Indians would be in for a surprise.

William Shirley, governor of Massachusetts, was about to spring one. In 1745 he fashioned a scheme for his colony rivaling anything Frontenac ever attempted. Shirley and Massachusetts leaders eyed the French fortress at Louisbourg, on Cape Breton, the barrier to the St. Lawrence River. (See Map No. 2, pp. 40–41.)

France had been a quarter of a century building Louisbourg. Huge blocks of granite for its walls had been shipped from Europe, as well as heavy and powerful cannon. Between five and six million dollars had gone into making Louisbourg "the Gibraltar of the New World."

French privateers from the fortress's fine harbor swooped down on British and American ships, capturing them as prizes. Bostonians were also hurt in the pocketbook when French fishermen, with backing from Louisbourg, began to net codfish in New England waters.

A rumor floated around New England that the Gibraltar of the New World had 250 cannon and 4,000 soldiers. But the clue to capturing this colossus in the north lay in the answer to the question "How determined are its defenders?" Governor Shirley thought he knew the answer.

CHAPTER 3

GOVERNOR SHIRLEY'S GAMBLE

GOVERNOR SHIRLEY's long nose twitched with excitement as he unfolded his intrepid scheme. Men of the General Court of Massachusetts sat entranced because Shirley exhibited the confidence of a master mariner steering his ship through dangerous waters. Shirley always thought he had the answer.

English-born William Shirley had moved to Boston in 1731, at the age of thirty-six. Colonial governors, like Shirley, were still being appointed by the Crown. Later, local-born men were appointed to this key position.

It was January, 1745, with dirty snow banked high in the Boston streets. In the courtroom, a smoky fire bothered most of the legislators, but not nearly as much as Shirley's fantastic plan. Some of the lawgivers shuddered. They knew the governor was not a careful planner.

William Shirley asked the legislators to rise and take an oath of secrecy. No one else must know of this plan, he warned forcefully—although word of conditions inside the French fortress at Louisbourg had drifted around New England. Shirley reminded the politicians that many citizens wanted Louisbourg captured. He talked of the French raid of the previous year that had wrecked the Canso fishing station, seventy miles south of Louisbourg. "In reality," he said, "their attack was poorly handled." He wagged a finger. "And I tell you the French also erred in letting our prisoners see the inside of Louisbourg. I personally questioned three of our men soon after they returned from imprisonment." Shirley was not a military leader, yet he went on unfolding plans for his gamble as if he were Hannibal.

He read aloud a private letter he had written the legislators:

. . . Louisbourg can be taken by surprise. . . . The more I consider the proposed Expedition the more I am persuaded three thousand men would remain Masters of the Field against the enemy. . . .

Originally Governor Shirley had said that two thousand men could capture Louisbourg. He skipped explaining how the fortress could be surprised.

Shirley went on to say expansively that one of the three men he had queried, John Bradstreet, a most unusual man, reported that the fortress did not have 250 cannon but 116, not 4,000 soldiers but 700. The governor

"Portrait of William Shirley,
Governor of Massachusetts."
Painting by Thomas Hudson.
*Courtesy Wadsworth
Atheneum, Hartford*

adjusted his wig and quoted Captain Bradstreet: "The morale of the French soldiers is at low tide. They hate the gloomy, cheerless fort, overrun by rats." Shirley related how, not long ago, the French soldiers had mutinied, and that they were often drunk. This seemed an invitation too good to overlook.

Shirley also quoted another of the three prisoners, William Vaughan, a Harvard graduate from Damariscotta, Maine. Vaughan had insisted that the capture of Louisbourg would not only revenge Canso, but would put New England fishermen in a stronger position to haul in greater tonnage of cod. Vaughan was heavily involved in the fishing industry, and if fishing boomed, Shirley himself would gain because the colony would prosper. Cod were gold from the sea. They were exchanged for needs of the New

Englanders: meat, flour, sugar, guns, ammunition, linen, molasses, wines, rum, and other articles.

In addition, Shirley had long dreamed that Canada would be part of New England. If he could accomplish this, in addition to safeguarding and bolstering the fishing business, he would become famous and rich. The first step was obvious: capture Louisbourg.

Ten years after Shirley's emigration from London, he had become governor of the Massachusetts Bay Colony. His desire to lead was a lash driving him on and on. The average day found this dynamo at his desk at sunrise, and he did not put away his quill and papers until midnight. He was able, possessed a charming personality, and looked like a successful school principal.

He ramrodded his scheme to take Louisbourg through the legislature by one vote.

Another of his acquaintances also determined to capture the French fortress was William Pepperrell. This wealthy and popular merchant from Kittery Point, Maine, like Shirley wore a white wig, but dressed even more fancily, affecting a flashy coat and waistcoat dotted with brass buttons, and he carried a cane. Pepperrell had a delightful personality. He liked people and people liked to be around him. It was a stroke of genius on Shirley's part to place Pepperrell in command of the expedition and to send Vaughan along.

Shirley's written directions to Pepperrell covered every possible point. The smartest thing in the maze of instructions was the statement that William Pepperrell could use his discretion. This Pepperrell did. He took the volunteers from Massachusetts, Connecticut, Rhode Island, and New Hampshire—raw militia—and made them realize that victory hinged on discipline. He also made them forget the differences and jealousies inherent in the makeup of the various colonies.

To get the expedition moving, Shirley levied several taxes and issued about $200,000 worth of paper money. In addition, he wrote His Majesty's naval leader, Commodore Warren, asking for man-of-war escort. It was common knowledge in the colonies that the British military looked down on colonial soldiers, but Pepperrell's shrewdness and friendliness impressed Commodore Warren, and Warren himself was anxious to cooperate in order to win.

The amateur colonial army of about 3,600 struggled ashore in April, 1745, assisted by the guns of Warren's four powerful warships. Vaughan led his men against a key defensive battery, found no one there, hoisted a red uniform jacket as a signal to Pepperrell, and then turned the guns of the battery against the French. A Bostonian, Lieutenant Colonel Richard Gridley, directed red-hot artillery shot into the town enclosed by the fortress.

After a siege of seven weeks, the French surrendered, and Pepperrell's "army" marched into the stinking, dismal fort and its town. The Reverend Samuel Moody, one of Pepperrell's Protestant chaplains, went to work swinging an ax, which he carried for the purpose, against religious images and the altar in the Catholic church. Not all the religious fanatics were on the French side.

When a sloop sailed into Boston and brought news of the victory, church bells rang. It was an amazing accomplishment by amateur soldiers, helped by irresolution of the French. Louisbourg cost the colonists 130 men dead. France lost 50. Then disease—dysentery—set in, and 1,500 Yankees became seriously ill.

When London heard of the capture, saluting guns in the Tower and the nearby park thundered. Pepperrell was created baronet and appointed a colonel. Shirley also became a colonel.

Good fortune for the Redcoats and provincials sailed into Louisbourg Harbor. French sea captains had not received news of the fall of the fortress. When they steered their ships into the harbor, Commodore Warren seized them, and he and his officers and men divided the prize money resulting from the captures. Warren's share amounted to what would be over a half million dollars today. The New Englanders got nothing. This was a bitter pill for Pepperrell and some of their leaders who had plunged deeply into debt to prepare the expedition. Pepperrell kept his men from declaring war on the Royal Navy, but British tars coming ashore were in danger of getting their heads punched.

In America the glamour of the victory quickly dimmed. New Englanders worried for fear Commodore Warren would push Pepperrell into the background, and bickering set in. New Hampshire men complained that Pepperrell was treating them unjustly. Then, when British ships carrying wounded sailed into Boston Harbor, the British sent "press gangs" from the warships to haul in seamen to serve in the King's ships. The colonial soldiers who were left to garrison Louisbourg became gloomy over their pay, or lack of it. Worse, nine hundred of them died during the bitter winter.

The French tried to retake the place, but their attacking fleet was defeated by storms and a plague. An English squadron turned back the next attempt.

Then a bombshell exploded. A ship brought word to

Boston in March, 1749, of the signing of the Treaty of
Aix-la-Chapelle in Germany on October 18, 1748. Under
the terms of this treaty, which ended the War of the Austrian Succession in Europe, Louisbourg and Cape Breton
were returned to the French.

New Englanders, including Governor Shirley, thought
the treaty outrageous. They were disgusted. The news was
hard to believe. Shirley's dream of making Canada part of
New England now died.

Britain sent almost a million dollars to America to help
Shirley with the expenses of the expedition, but this did not
salve New Englanders' feelings over Commodore Warren's greed or over the return of Louisbourg, a fortress
gained and lost. Once again French ships would be able
to swoop down from the north to interfere with New
England fishermen.

The capture and siege of Louisbourg in 1745 was an
incident of the spasmodic border warfare that raged for
over fifty years, marked by cruel raids, massacres, torture,
and enslavement of captives, a war of close combat—the
tomahawk, scalping knife, and short-range musket. (See
Appendix I for summaries of these wars.) The border
conflict continued to smolder. How could a treaty
signed an ocean away settle it? And for years, Indians of
the Northeast could not understand why the British had
returned Louisbourg to the French.

CHAPTER 4

TRADE AND TRICKERY

I N misty morning light, two Mohawks pounded their tomahawks against the palisade gate. Instantly, two soldiers popped up like jack-in-the-boxes in the lookout hatches on the roof.

The soldiers aimed their muskets at the gate. The guns and the pointed, twelve-foot-high palisade guarding William Johnson's newly built gray stone house suggested a fort. Heavy oak shutters and massive doors completed the picture. But in 1754 it was also a beautiful house, forty miles east of Albany, New York.

The Indians howled like wild dogs. One shouted, "Warragh-i-ya-gey!"

When the two Indians had been identified as friends, they were brought into the house. Johnson boomed a welcome as he received them in his spacious living room, his voice sounding like a trumpet in a well.

Johnson tossed split birch logs on the embers in the fireplace, and in a moment red sparks crackled out, reflecting on the polished black walnut paneling. In another moment, the fire sputtered and popped, then ran across the top of the logs and spread to partially burned kindling.

Johnson threw open a shutter to see better the cylindrical shells in the wampum the Indians had given him. He praised them, then put the belt away carefully in a cherrywood highboy recently arrived from England. He poured the two visitors tiny glasses of Madeira wine. A Negro slave removed a chess set from a drop-leaf table and placed a dish of warmed-over pickerel on it. The fish had been fried in yellow cornmeal. The Mohawks grabbed handfuls and crammed it into their mouths. One sputtered at Johnson, "My brother, we have bad news."

The Indian pushed more fish into his mouth and said the French were on the rise, that it had been a big mistake to have given them back the big, big fort near the mouth of the St. Lawrence, six years before. He warned that next month thirty canoes carrying five hundred Canadian Indians would paddle down the Ohio, advance guard for six thousand French and Indians. He finished in a shout, "They will build forts along that stream!"

William Johnson believed. He trusted Indians, particularly Mohawks, the leading tribe of the Six Nation Iroquois Confederacy—a well-knit organization including Oneidas, Onondagas, Cayugas, Senecas, and the Tuscaroras of North Carolina. Johnson liked to say he had given hundreds of Indians credit to buy things, and he had always been repaid unless the Indian was killed and could not pay his debt.

The Mohawks had made Johnson a chief, naming him War-ragh-i-ya-gey. He translated this as "a man who undertakes great things." Others said the jaw-breaking title meant "superintendent of affairs." Some Indians called the powerful trader "Mr. Big Business." He was indeed that.

To the Iroquois, Johnson seemed part of the Six Nations. He was genuinely interested in them, and when he was Indian agent, he had administered their affairs with wisdom. When his wife died, he married an Indian maiden. He had fathered half-breed children, to the disgust of the white community in Albany. Johnson spoke the Mohawk tongue, and at times daubed paint on his face, pulling on buckskins and a headdress to dance with his brothers around council fires. William Johnson, almost six feet tall and with a powerful chest, had a placid face masking his ambition, shrewdness, capacity to hate, vanity, and drive.

The Iroquois respected him. He gave Indians a square deal when they traded furs for guns, ammunition, cloth, pots and pans, fishhooks, and other things. His prices were nailed to the stockade for all to see. This smart leader had become one of the most powerful white men in America.

Johnson listened carefully to the two Mohawks as they gulped the fish. His blue eyes snapped as they talked of the enemy. He thanked them, promised them presents after they had eaten, and said he would convey their valuable information to British leaders meeting in Albany in June.

The Mohawks expected this—talk, talk, conferences, and meetings—although their own chief, King Hendrick, wanted a conference. There would be rum and presents.

Johnson considered the problem. The Six Nations held the balance of power in northeastern America, and knew it. They had a background of war, not only because they liked to fight but because they were determined to control the fur trade. Trade in furs brought things they needed. The British supplied these more cheaply than the French, and British goods were better made. Also, British rum was more powerful than French brandy and cost less.

Rules of trade meant little to the powerful Iroquois middlemen. Their country lay astride principal trade routes; one had to pay a toll in furs to bring pelts through Iroquois country. In addition, they even smuggled furs into Canada, in spite of French regulations.

The Mohawk River stretched across upper New York. It was an avenue for furs coming from the west to the beautiful Hudson, a street that led to New York City and Europe.

The Iroquois guarded their part of the fur trade jealously, because they had to govern it to survive. Once when *coureurs de bois* (French backwoodsmen who preferred the Indian way of life to humdrum existence in towns) and western Indians diverted furs from the Mohawk River to the St. Lawrence, the Iroquois went on the warpath. They killed all the *coureurs de bois* they could find. Huron villages were set on fire and their young warriors burned at the stake. Huron women, old men, and children were enslaved. The Eries received the same harsh treatment. The Iroquois, motivated by over a hun-

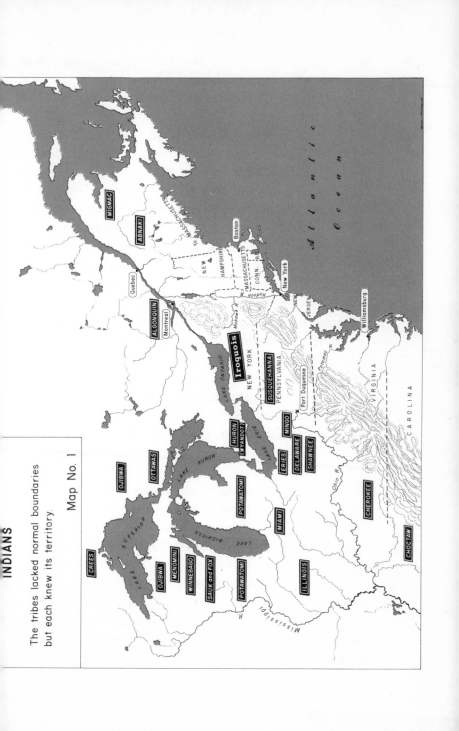

INDIANS

The tribes lacked normal boundaries but each knew its territory.

Map No. 1

CREES

OJIBWA

OJIBWA

OTTAWAS

MENOMINI

WINNEBAGO

SAULK and FOX

POTAWATOMI

POTAWATOMI

HURON (WYANDOT)

MIAMI

ILLINOIS

ERIES

MINGO

DELAWARE

SHAWNEE

MIGMAC

ABNAKI

ALGONQUIN

Iroquois

SUSQUEHANNA

CHEROKEE

CHOCTAW

Atlantic Ocean

Quebec

Montreal

Boston

New York

Williamsburg

Fort Duquesne

NEW YORK

PENNSYLVANIA

NEW JERSEY

VIRGINIA

CAROLINA

MASSACHUSETTS

NEW HAMPSHIRE

MASSACHUSETTS

CONN.

LAKE SUPERIOR

LAKE HURON

LAKE MICHIGAN

LAKE ERIE

LAKE ONTARIO

MISSISSIPPI R.

Ohio R.

Potomac R.

Hudson R.

Mohawk R.

dred years of governing the fur trade, brooked no interference.

The Iroquois fighter-traders, particularly Mohawks, had helped the British when they feared French soldiers were headed for New York—not for love of the British but to keep the fur trade in line the way they wanted. Then when Frenchmen tried to circumvent Iroquois tentacles by sending fleets of canoes, manned by French *voyageurs*, to deliver furs, the Iroquois attacked the canoe men.

The French did not quit easily. They sent blacksmiths into the forest to woo the Iroquois by making articles of iron the Indians needed. Some chiefs were given French uniforms and medals. Faithful Jesuits, the advance guard of French civilization, tried to Christianize the Iroquois but with little success. A Jesuit reported to his superior, "The Iroquois are subtle, adroit, wandering knaves." And the Indians complained to the British, "The Jesuits knock in our barrel heads and pour rum on the ground." For a good reason: the Indians seemed unable to drink alcohol in moderation.

The Indians knew the French dreamed of connecting their settlements on the St. Lawrence with those at the mouth of the Mississippi. Before 1754, Iroquois brought in lead plates the French had buried in the forests, and the British took pains to explain the disks represented French claims on their lands.

The Iroquois saw themselves in a vise that was ever tightening. On one hand, if the French were successful, Iroquois routes west would be cut. This was indeed a worry. On the other hand, British craving for land bothered the Indians. Still another prospect haunted the Iroquois: an alliance between the British and French with the purpose of defeating them. To the Six Nations, the best solution to their worries was warfare between the British and French, with each side wearing the other down. The Iroquois had a consuming desire to be on the side of the winners.

Iroquois were not the only ones in America who were afraid. The French in Canada numbered about sixty thousand, and they worried because British power was growing in America. King George II had approximately a half million more or less loyal American subjects.

The French in America had severe problems. They suffered because the dissolute King Louis XV spent money like a crazy man, wasting much of it on European wars. He was not interested in colonization in America, but in furs, women, clothes, and palaces.

The British colonies had a limited horizon. They were independent and jealous of each other. Their traders had a worry: When they pushed across the Alleghenies, they saw the French threatening their trade with the Indians. In British towns along the coast, most people were involved with commerce that depended on ships, and all but a few had forgotten what an Indian in war paint looked like.

Some of the colonists saw the problem of the Indians. One of these, Peter Wraxall, secretary to William Johnson, wrote: "Trade is the only Method [by which we can] overthrow French influence among the Indians."

He also realized the predicament of the Iroquois when he penned a memorandum:

> To preserve the Ballance between us & the French is the great ruling Principle of Modern Indian Politics. [They know] trade is the foundation of their Alliance

THE COLONIES AND KEY FORTS
BEFORE AND DURING THE WAR

Boundaries indefinite

SCALE OF MILES

Map No. 2

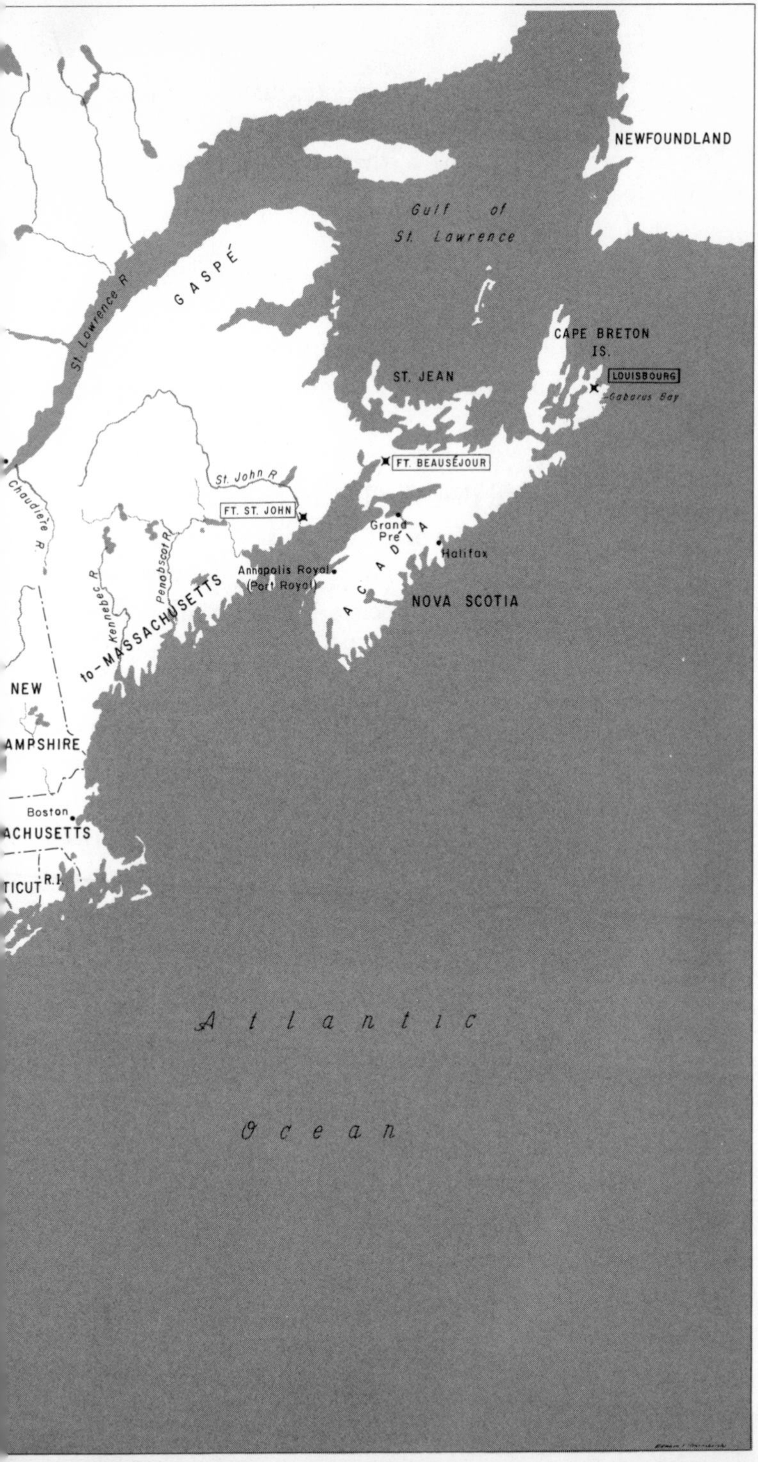
NEWFOUNDLAND
Gulf of
St. Lawrence
GASPÉ
St. Lawrence R.
CAPE BRETON
IS.
LOUISBOURG
Gabarus Bay
ST. JEAN
FT. BEAUSÉJOUR
St. John R.
Chaudière R.
FT. ST. JOHN
Grand
Pré
Halifax
ACADIA
Annapolis Royal
(Port Royal)
NOVA SCOTIA
Kennebec R.
Penobscot R.
to-MASSACHUSETTS
NEW
AMPSHIRE
Boston
ACHUSETTS
R.I.
TICUT
Atlantic
Ocean

or Connexions with us & that this is the chief Cement W^{en} binds us together.

William Penn's secretary put it more simply: "If we lose the Iroquois we are gone."

By 1754 William Penn had been dead thirty-six years. His thoughts, however, were as good as when he wrote them:

I am apprehensive that the Indian trade will involve us in some fatal quarrel with the Indians. Our traders, in defiance of the law, carrying liquors to the Indians, take advantage of their appetite for it, cheating them of their skins and wampum and debauching their wives.

It was against these turbulent currents that twenty-three outstanding men met in Albany at the invitation of Lieutenant Governor James DeLancey of New York. The idea: to control Indian affairs. They arrived from Massachusetts, Rhode Island, Connecticut, New Hampshire, Maryland, Pennsylvania. Lieutenant Governor Robert Dinwiddie of Virginia sent no one, as he was busy treating the French and Indians in his own way.

A leading character at the conference was the Mohawk political wizard, King Hendrick, so named by the Dutch. Hendrick was about seventy, small and stocky, with a shaven head, and he wore a lace shirt with a red blanket draped over his shoulders. Hendrick was not awed by British representatives. The old chief had traveled twice to London. Not even his friend Johnson, an Irishman, had seen that city.

As King Hendrick talked, he fingered the tomahawk

in his belt. This small ax had thirty-nine "X's." "Each cross," Hendrick liked to boast, "is a man I killed in battle."

Hendrick reminded the men in the conference room of the help the Iroquois, especially the Mohawks, had given in the past. He accused the colonists of failing to protect their own interests. He talked of "cowardly desertion of traders from the Oswego trading post that has upset Indians of the west." The chief was speaking more truthfully than the petty, small-time New York Lieutenant Governor DeLancey, who refused to admit Indians had ever been right in anything.

"Tell us," King Hendrick barked, "what you will do about the French in the lakes and in the Ohio Valley, or tell us you will do nothing for us."

Meanwhile, before the representatives and the Indians met in conference in Albany, Governor Dinwiddie of Virginia had sent a young militia leader into the forests on an extremely perilous mission.

CHAPTER 5

MAJOR WASHINGTON
IN THE FOREST

WHEN a packhorse plodded over a ledge of rock cresting above the snow, the clatter thudded through the Virginia forest like drumbeats. Major George Washington motioned back to the four fur traders to move the animals to softer footing. The Half King aimed his musket at a thicket on a hillside, then, when he was sure it was harmless, ran to catch up with Washington, who was walking a hundred yards behind the handful of Indians in the advance guard. The Seneca chief had been doing this all morning because each mile traveled increased the danger of ambush. This was late 1753.

The Half King, about fifty, was a shrewd and vigorous Indian who loved rum and flattery and despised the French.

He often said bitterly, "The French boiled and ate my father."

Hiking ahead of the Half King and Washington was Christopher Gist, alert frontiersman. Gist's moral force, knowledge of the country, and ability to speak Indian tongues were tremendous aids to the twenty-one-year-old major. Gist, a surveyor for the Ohio Company of Virginia, was present on this perilous trek into the wilds at the request of Governor Dinwiddie. The Virginia governor was personally interested and involved in the Ohio Company.

Washington depended on Gist and the Half King, although at times the Indian chief was totally irresponsible. Gist, however, not only knew the way to Fort Venango— the main trail to the Ohio—but he had the zeal of a missionary. He once held Protestant religious services for the Indians in what would some day become Ohio. Another valuable aide on the march was the Dutchman Jacob van Braam, who could speak both English and French.

Merciless rain drenched the small party. Washington's buckskin jacket, reaching to his knees, seemed to weigh a ton. Worse, the rain made the baggage, heaped on the wretched pack animals, heavier. How long could they keep going?

When Washington ordered a halt, half of the animals sank to the ground as if they would never arise. It was hard to start them. This worried him. The corn for the horses was carried in the packs, and each animal needed it if he were to carry food and tents for the men plodding along with Washington toward the French fort. Each tortuous mile seemed harder than the last.

Washington had volunteered for this mission. What the odds were that he could travel from Williamsburg to Fort

Venango and back in dead of winter, no one could say. He checked the waterproof packet inside his hunting shirt. The tallow-coated buckskin envelope carried Dinwiddie's message warning the French that, if harmony was to exist between the two nations, the French must leave the Ohio Valley.

On December 4, 1753, the travelers stopped at the edge of a clearing. A small log-and-mud fort squatted in its center. From the flagpole the French fleur-de-lis flapped in the cold wind as if to say, "We French are here to stay." It was almost dusk.

Captain de Joncaire, commandant at Fort Venango, received Major Washington with icy reserve threaded with courtesy. Washington, over six feet tall, watched the swarthy, half-French, half-Seneca leader as the inter-

"George Washington When He Wore the King's Coat." Copied by John Gadsby Chapman from an original painting by Charles Willson Peale.

Courtesy West Point Museum Collections

preter read aloud Governor Dinwiddie's message. Joncaire studied it, his brow knit as if the message were Greek. He shrugged and handed it back to Washington. "You must take this to my headquarters, Commandant Washington, at Fort Le Boeuf."

"How much farther is that?" Washington asked.

"About fifty miles."

Before supper, Washington pulled on his uniform. Captain de Joncaire poured wine for Major Washington and the French officers from the meager supply in the fort. Several glasses made Joncaire talkative. That night in his tent George Washington wrote in his journal:

The Wine, as the French dosed themselves plentifully, loosened their tongues. They told me it was their absolute Design to take possession of the Ohio, and by G—— they would do it. They pretend to claim the country from a Discovery by one La Salle. . . .

Washington knew the Virginia charter went back to 1609 and that British traders had crossed the Alleghenies for years. La Salle may have reached the Ohio River in 1669.

The French in the little fort downed their wine, and without a show of guile tried to win over Washington's Indians with presents and alcohol. The Half King helped Washington but because of the pull of the French they were barely able to march their party away from the fort two days later on the miserable trail to Fort Le Boeuf.

The weather worsened. Icy winds lashed the party. The fifty miles seemed harder than the long climb over the lonely barrier ridges of the Alleghenies. Few settlers had crossed the wooded slopes; the country, guarded by hills and misty peaks, was a land of mystery. The packhorses grew weaker. After swimming an icy stream the animals refused to go on, and the fur traders could make them go only by beating them. Nevertheless, Washington and Gist brought the party straggling into Fort Le Boeuf in four days—for Washington it was the end of a tortuous four-hundred-mile trip.

A blind man could see that the French at Fort Le Boeuf were not only there to stay but were planning to travel downstream. Supplies lay heaped on both sides of the stockade. About two hundred canoes were lined up on the narrow beaches of the river like tents in a formal camp, and *voyageurs* were building more canoes. In addition, Captain Saint-Pierre, who welcomed Washington, had the confident air of a landowner. He received Dinwiddie's message, then retired to write his answer. It took him three days. His reply was a firm No. The French were in Ohio for keeps.

When George Washington headed his party away from the fort, his Indians delayed him. Some disappeared into the forest. Washington's appeals to the Half King brought only the laconic reply, "They have gone hunting." Washington waited a day and was rewarded, because the Indians brought back three bears.

It became colder. Snow fell, and frostbitten hands and feet became a serious hazard. Gist suffered frostbite in all his fingers and in some of his toes. Washington narrowly escaped drowning when an accident threw him from a raft into an ice-clogged stream. Then the Indian carrying his pack asked for Washington's rifle. When Washington refused, the Indian grew surly. This guide, working under

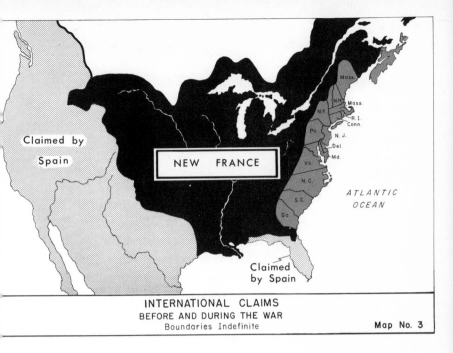

Claimed by
Spain

NEW FRANCE

Claimed
by Spain

Mass.
N.H. Mass.
N.Y. R.I.
Conn.
Pa. N.J.
Del.
Md.
Va.
N.C.
S.C.
Ga.

ATLANTIC
OCEAN

INTERNATIONAL CLAIMS
BEFORE AND DURING THE WAR
Boundaries Indefinite

Map No. 3

Gist, insisted on taking a direction Gist felt was wrong. After some talk, and without warning, the Indian fired at Washington or Gist. Neither was hit. They made a prisoner of the Indian and released him the next day.

It took Washington a month to ride from Fort Le Boeuf into Williamsburg—good time in the dead of winter. Travel in North America, except in colonial towns, was over cowpaths that could not be dignified by the name of roads, or along dim forest trails. This made rivers of great importance as travel arteries. Today it is hard to visualize the difficulty of travel in eighteenth-century North America. And on the Atlantic it took a sailing ship a month to reach Europe—longer if winds blew unfavorably.

Washington ended his dangerous trip on January 16, 1754, when he handed the French commandant's reply to the bulky, benevolent governor. Dinwiddie listened carefully to Washington and pondered the note. A few weeks later the governor, braced by messages from London, wrote:

A Proclamation

For Encouraging *Men* to enlist in His Majesty's Service for the Defense & Security of this Colony.

Whereas . . . a fort must be immediately built on the River *Ohio*, at the Fork of the Monongahela to stop hostile attempts of the French & Indians . . .

[The proclamation went on to promise land on the Ohio to volunteers whose "Good Behaviour and Service shall deserve it." It was signed:]

At the Council Chamber, in Williamsburg, the 19th day of February, 1754,

Robert Dinwiddie
GOD save the KING

Dinwiddie penned letters to other colonial governors pleading with them to act with him—quickly—but his pleas met with apathy. New York's reply was influenced by fur traders. There was no reason to act now that furs were coming into New York. "Maybe later," the New Yorkers said. Quakers in Pennsylvania saw no reason to fight. The other colonies were "busy," except North Carolina, which voted money and a few soldiers. Because of the situation, the British government ordered one of its "Independent Companies" of regular soldiers from South Carolina to Virginia.

The Ohio Company reacted to Washington's news by building a crude palisade fence around a log storehouse at the magnificent Forks of the Ohio. They called it Fort Prince George, although it was a poor excuse for a fort.

One company of Virginia militia marched toward the fort.

In came the French and forced surrender of the half-built stockade. Up went a better fort, on or near the site of Fort Prince George, which they christened Fort Duquesne. The Forks became a very important place.

When Dinwiddie heard of the French move, he was furious. As soon as he recovered his composure, he sent Washington, now a lieutenant colonel, at the head of soldiers toward the Forks. Target: Fort Duquesne.

George Washington was a complex individual, but he now had a singleness of purpose as staunch as Governor Dinwiddie's. Both believed the future of the country lay in a solution of the problem centered at the Forks. Both believed it imperative that the French be forced to leave the Ohio River Valley.

Although Washington was well aware of the short-comings of his Virginia volunteers and the South Carolina Independent Company (about 150 dissolute and aged regulars from the British Army), he was determined to defeat the enemy. With him were a number of Indians. He did not have an impressive force.

En route Washington received the bad news of the surrender of Fort Prince George, as well as a warning note from the Half King, obviously written with help:

TO THE FORIST OF HIS MAJESTIES
OFFIVERSES THIS MEAY CONCERN

[IT IS REPORTED] THE FRENCH ARMY IS SET OUT TO MEET MIGER GEORG WASHINGTON I DEESIRE YOU TO BE AWAR OF THEM. . . . I WILL BE WITH YOU IN FIVE DAYS TO CONSEL. . . .

Soon after receiving this, Washington built a tiny, make-shift defense work, naming it Fort Necessity. He called the site (near modern Elliottsville, Pennsylvania) Great Meadows.

While Washington was working to improve the trail toward Fort Duquesne, the Half King and some of his Indians arrived with bad news.

"French on the way," the Half King told Washington. "Their leader—a young man, de Jumonville."

Washington acted. He led a small detachment of soldiers and the Half King's Indians against de Jumonville and defeated him on May 28, 1754. De Jumonville was killed.

Washington now stopped work on the road. Reinforcements swelled his party to almost four hundred men. But they were poorly trained and more than a quarter of them were sick. Nevertheless, in his determined way, Washington led his meager force on toward Fort Duquesne. When scouts arrived saying that a larger French force was coming through the woods toward him, the Half King and his Indians oozed out of sight into the forest. Washington fell back to Fort Necessity.

The French, about six hundred soldiers and Canadian *voyageurs* and a hundred Indians, smashed out of the forest in three columns against the tiny fort. Louis de Villiers was the leader of the attack. As forceful as he was, he could not bring all of his Canadian Indians into the fight. Most of them howled on the sidelines, watching.

In a nine-hour, unequal battle, most of it in the rain, the French overpowered the defenders. Major Robert Stobo, one of Washington's defenders, capsuled the story of the short siege: "George Washington led men who were self-willed and almost ungovernable."

The French treated the defeated Washington and his men generously. Indians from Canada yelled for scalps, but the French restrained them. After French and Indians plundered Fort Necessity, two French soldiers and one Indian, along with about thirteen men who had fought under Washington, were buried.

Washington had to sign articles of surrender, then march his men away as a drummer tapped out time. But the French had been crafty. At their request, he had signed the articles at dark in the rain, with the aid of a flickering candle, not knowing what he was signing because of a poor translation. These papers said he had assassinated young de Jumonville. Later the French used this as propaganda.

Before letting Washington go, they forced him to leave two hostages to ensure that certain prisoners of the British would be returned. For this unenviable assignment, Washington chose his Dutch interpreter and a most unusual Scot, temporary resident of Virginia, Major Robert Stobo. This soldier was dedicated to escaping from the French.

Stobo, of course, was one individual against a huge backdrop. The musketry rattling at Fort Necessity eventually pitted England against France in the Seven Years' War, really the fourth worldwide war they had fought in less than a century. In America, the fight at Fort Necessity started the French and Indian War, battles of intense close combat. The prize was tremendous: most of the North American continent.

CHAPTER 6

POLITICS IN ALBANY

WHILE muskets popped in the rain at Fort Necessity, the conference in Albany was still struggling along, accomplishing little.

In the Albany courthouse during that summer of 1754, Lieutenant Governor James DeLancey of New York presided at the head of the table. Colonel William Johnson, the successful Indian trader, sat close by with twenty-three colonial conferees along the sides. Iroquois chiefs, in finest buckskins and ornaments, sat at the foot. The Indians possessed an advantage over the white men: the Iroquois knew what they wanted.

The Mohawk King Hendrick rose with dignity after a nod of recognition. "You talk, talk against the French taking our lands," the old chief rasped, "but you grab land in Virginia, in Penn's Land, and here in New York.

The French tell us many times, 'If you don't fight the English, they will drive you forever from your hunting grounds.' Many of our people wonder who is right."

The chief pointed out that French traders took Indian wives, that the English did not, "except for our dear friend Johnson."

King Hendrick also protested that British traders hurt the tribes by bringing too much rum rather than things they needed badly—pots, blankets, hatchets, and guns. In a half shout he said, "Albany traders sell arms to the French, while you tell us to fight them. Why is this? Here we meet in the ancient place of treaty where fires of friendship used to burn. You have not asked us to smoke with you. Signs are not right. The French are men prepared to fight. We are ashamed. Where are your fortifications?"

Hendrick's brother Abraham spoke of the faith the Iroquois placed in Colonel Johnson and said that in the three years since Johnson had laid aside the management of Indian affairs in New York, because of white men's politics, the Iroquois had become uneasy. Abraham went on, "We lay down this belt [of wampum] before all brethren present and want Colonel Johnson again to have our management. We love him and he us." Then Abraham finished with all the irony he could command, "We think our request about Johnson, which we made before and which we were told was forwarded to the King, our father, has been sunk in the sea."

Speeches by the two Indians stopped the conference while the conferees argued what to do.

After several days, back came the Indians. Johnson lessened the tension by talking to them in his loud voice and persuasive way. He understood Indians and backed them. He told them he *wanted* a military campaign. With this, part of the political conference ended, after land along the Susquehanna River in Pennsylvania was purchased from the Indians. The Iroquois then left for their homes, partly satisfied but complaining that the thirty wagonloads of gifts, rumbling along behind them, could have included more useful items.

After the Indians left, the leading spirit of the conference unfolded his plan. He was almost fifty. He sported a maroon waistcoat over his portly stomach, a neat white ruffle on his shirt bosom, and brass buckles on his shoes. Spectacles from England sat on his nose, because he had to put up with poor eyesight. By this time in his remarkable life, he had established himself as a writer, printer, publisher, inventor, administrator, politician, and a natural philosopher—who experimented with "electrical fire and electrical guns." He was the foremost American political thinker of his century. This was, of course, the man later called "the first civilized American," Benjamin Franklin.

Franklin, in his rare, confident manner, proposed two ideas: a general treaty with the Indians instead of numerous separate ones, and that the colonies join in a perpetual union. All knew of his woodcut, published in his *Pennsylvania Gazette*, showing a separated snake, each part marked with the name of a colony. The cartoon bore the caption "JOIN, or DIE." It had more force than a cannonball.

Franklin was handicapped because he was not a persuasive speaker. However, he had no equal in working behind the scenes, and the conferees adopted his "Plan of

"Join, or Die." Woodcut by Benjamin Franklin, from *The Pennsylvania Gazette*, May 9, 1754.
Courtesy of the New York Historical Society, New York City

Union." Thomas Hutchinson of Massachusetts contributed to it. Some liked one feature, some another, but all agreed that immediate joint defense measures were a necessity.

They had good reason to think so because a month after the conference began, Caughnawagas, "Praying Indians," ransacked "Dutch Hoosick," in upper New York, firing homes and barns and killing herds of cattle. When shocked settlers walked into Albany half naked, carrying what belongings they had managed to save, they were living proof that better defense measures were needed—and fast. The savages tore across northern New York, spreading like a cloud of dust, putting the torch to another settlement, then striking in New Hampshire.

In view of this, and as part of his Plan of Union, Franklin proposed a "common army." "We must unite," he

said, "to defeat the common enemy." His Plan of Union
was a smart form for improved living, but it was disapproved by the various colonies because they feared loss
of independence. It was also rejected in England because
the idea of giving colonials their own army and too much
responsibility and authority was definitely obnoxious.

Franklin's fault was that he was ahead of his time.
Years later, it was recognized that his plan set down principles that became part of the American political system.
Although the conference failed, it is a landmark in
history.

Before the conferees traveled home, word arrived of
the crumbling Virginia frontier. It shook Albany. Governor Shirley of Massachusetts had already ordered active
measures for the defense of his border country. Colonel
Israel Williams, experienced soldier of Louisbourg days,
had persuaded the governor that groups of rangers
should be formed—"men skilled in woodcraft and bush
fighting, to meet the enemy on their own ground." Forts
were strengthened with cannon, and a chain of forts was
built connecting with those in New York.

Even stuffy and sluggish politicians in London eventually reacted to the outbreak of massacres and burnings.
The idea developed that the colonies would furnish recruits, houses to be used as barracks, horses, forage, and
wagons, and would chip in to a common defense fund.

His Majesty's Government would send to America
professional soldiers with a major general commanding.
The general selected was Edward Braddock, who would
become one of the most unjustly criticized generals in
history.

CHAPTER 7

GENERAL BRADDOCK'S TROUBLES

B RADDOCK *did* have a nasty temper. British author and politician Horace Walpole wrote, "Braddock is a very Iroquois in disposition."

But Braddock had his dreams. He was sixty, with forty-five years in His Majesty's service. The regiment he had been raised in and loved as an Army boy, the famous Coldstream Guards, was almost his religion. Although the Guards had seen much front-line service, Braddock had continually been shunted to other assignments. However, he progressed upward from rank to rank, he made friends quickly, and he gained the reputation of being a disciplinarian, but fair.

At this time, the average British Army officer hated colonial service. Service across the Atlantic was generally regarded as duty at the end of the world. The West

Indies were pestholes, where fevers killed men by the hundreds; North America was an unknown wilderness where few British soldiers ever had served. But when Dinwiddie flooded overseas mail with appeals for help, someone had to go, and Braddock was chosen and promoted to major general. He did not argue or evade the assignment. That was not the way of the Coldstream Guards. This was his chance to command in combat, to gain praise from the King and his countrymen. General Braddock told close friends goodby and made his will. Did he have a premonition of impending disaster?

The King handed him eight pages of instructions, drawn up by his third son, the Duke of Cumberland, a conscientious soldier but a poor general. The orders covered everything except how to cook meat over a campfire. But they were definite on one point: Braddock was first to drive the French out of Fort Duquesne.

The French soldiers in Fort Duquesne, in Canada, and along the line of the French thrust into the heart of North America were as brave as any who ever marched onto a battlefield. They would be outnumbered in America, but they were determined fighters.

Braddock, however, knew his two understrength regiments were not powerful enough. He counted on colonials rallying to the colors.

When his ship dropped anchor in Hampton Roads, Virginia, in February, 1755, after a rough crossing of seven weeks, General Braddock shaved, pulled on his red coat, wound a blood-red sash around his fat stomach and sword belt, hooked on his sword, stepped into a longboat, and was rowed ashore to the new village of Hampton. A fresh breeze made him hang on to his lustrous, black, tricornered hat, crowned with gold lace.

The portly leader could still feel the roll of the deck as he walked by a fishmonger's in Hampton, where Negro slaves cleaned flounder and picked crabmeat.

In Williamsburg, Dinwiddie welcomed him to his pink two-story brick palace. The beautiful town with its William and Mary College seemed like a bit of old England. Braddock, at the governor's table, enjoyed delicious Chesapeake Bay oysters, cold crabmeat, baked ham and sweet potatoes, cornbread lathered with fresh butter, a new food to him—all washed down with sweet cider and Madeira wine. Life seemed as tranquil as the Palace Green stretching out from the palace, until Governor Dinwiddie talked of friction among the colonies.

This discord was Braddock's first blow. Two centuries later, Sir Winston Churchill described the lack of harmony between the colonies in one short sentence: "They were united in distrusting the Home Goverment but in little else." Braddock fretted. To succeed, he needed the cooperation of the colonies in furnishing recruits, supplies, horses, forage, and wagons. To make the picture blacker, Dinwiddie explained that, when the colonies were not quarreling with each other, the legislatures were feuding with their governors. Otherwise, Dinwiddie said, things were shaping up. He was delighted to have a British general who would run the French out of the Ohio Valley.

Dinwiddie now spread out on a Queen Anne table a most amazing piece of enemy intelligence. It was a neat drawing of Fort Duquesne by Major Stobo, one of the hostages Washington had left behind when the French overwhelmed him at Fort Necessity.

Robert Stobo's experiences are a real American adventure story. When he became a captive of the French, he gave his word not to escape, but he did not construe this as a bar to helping his adopted country. At the risk of his life, he drew a sketch of the defenses of Fort Duquesne, and gambled again when he hired an Indian named Moses to carry the map to the British. Stobo followed up with a letter about the fort, giving this to another Indian, Delaware George, to carry to his friends. It urged a British attack.

Later, after Braddock's defeat, the French captured the sketch and moved Stobo to a Quebec dungeon. He was tried and sentenced to be beheaded. But King Louis XV disapproved the court's decision. Stobo later became famous. He wrote his *Memoirs* in the third person, referring to himself, although modestly, as "Our Hero." This brave spirit kept his humor. He wrote of his imprisonment, "We find him in a dungeon, lying on a bed of straw, with a morsel of bread and a pan of cold water by his side, the cold earthen floor his table, no cheerful friend to pledge him a glass, or other guest came there, except a mouse ran past his meagre fare."

Two of Stobo's sentences, carried by Delaware George, burned in General Braddock's mind: "The Garrison at Fort Duquesne consists of 200 men. It will soon be 400." But what did "soon" mean?

After studying Stobo's information, the British leader decided he must haul heavy guns to overwhelm the fort, although the mountainous country lacked a road, and even though Stobo had added, "One hundred Indians can

take this place by surprize." One hundred Indians over-
power four hundred Frenchmen? Impossible. Braddock
received verifying information, a report from a soldier of
fortune, Thomas Forbes: "Fort Duquesne is manned by
400 men."

Braddock knew what four hundred determined defenders could do behind staunch ramparts. But when
Braddock thought of "forts," his ideas were European.
He imagined solid, carefully designed structures of ma-
sonry, with cannons laid precisely to cover fields of fire—
almost impenetrable defenses built by skilled engineer officers and craftsmen. Braddock could not visualize the
average flimsy frontier fort.

The general started on his perilous adventure by sending couriers galloping out of Williamsburg to summon
the governors for a conference at Annapolis, Maryland.
(Actually, the mounted messengers pulled down to a slow
trot after leaving the dust of the town behind; a horse can
travel at top speed for only short distances.)

General Braddock had been in America a little over a
month when he met the governors at Alexandria, Virginia,
and at Annapolis, Maryland. He took a quick liking to
Governor Shirley and in a surprise move appointed him
"second-in-command in America." This upset Lieutenant
Governor DeLancey and laid the foundation for bitter-
ness and jealousy among the colonial leaders.

The governors sent Braddock's temper skyrocketing
because they said they could not contribute to a common defense fund. Clearly, Braddock realized the colonies
wanted the enemy chased away, and peace and prosperity,
but they wanted the home government in London to
pay all expenses.

The conference went on. The idea was advanced that General Braddock would be wise to cut off the French closer to their source of supply: Quebec. But Braddock was not tampering with his orders.

Finally, he approved the strategy for the war. He would go ahead and take Fort Duquesne. (And he had secret instructions to push on, organizing a thrust against Niagara.) William Johnson would be colonel of the Six Nations and Indian agent. He would obtain Iroquois help and would attack the French at the southern end of Lake Champlain. Governor Shirley would cut through New York and Iroquois territory and attack Fort Niagara, between Lake Erie and Lake Ontario. At the same time, a long-anticipated expedition would strike Nova Scotia and settle the problem of the troublesome Acadians.

The principal leaders of these ambitious plans, Braddock, Shirley, and Johnson, had never been in combat. Braddock, however, was well trained. Shirley had engineered the successful campaign against Louisbourg, but the dust of ten years lay on those laurels. William Johnson knew the Iroquois, and a friendly feeling existed between him and their powerful tribes, but what kind of leader would he be at the head of a combat force?

Braddock told the governors forcefully that to capture Fort Duquesne he had to have more wagons than those he had brought with him from London—not for his men to ride in, but to carry food, forage for the horses, and hundreds of necessary supplies. The conferees promised, before departing, to send wagons, but in the next weeks precious few rumbled in.

While Braddock waited impatiently, a great American leader helped him. Benjamin Franklin impressed Braddock as one of the few Americans who could get action. Franklin advertised in Pennsylvania for wagons, got them, and breathed with relief when Braddock paid for them.

Benjamin Franklin wrote in his *Autobiography* that he told Braddock:

> . . . The only Danger for you is from Ambuscades of Indians. . . . And the slender Line near four Miles long, which your Army must make, may expose it to be attack'd by Surprize in its flanks, and to be cut like a Thread into several Pieces. [Braddock was] a brave Man, and might probably have made a Figure as a good Officer in some European War. But he had too much self-confidence, too high an Opinion of the Validity of Regular Troops, and too mean a One of both Americans and Indians. . . .

Franklin also tried to counsel Braddock on the route, but the general's mind was made up.

This part of the *Autobiography* was written thirty-three years after Braddock led his force through the forests. Franklin could remember that far back, but maybe not so precisely. He enjoyed writing entertainingly. For instance, he decorated his autobiography by inserting documents such as the list he had had his son draw up. It detailed supplies he sent into camp for young, low-ranking British officers who lacked money to buy delicacies:

6 lb. Loaf Sugar	1 Gloucester Cheese
1 lb. good Green Tea	2 Gallons Jamaica Spirits

6 lb. good ground Coffee	1 Kegg containing 20 lb.
6 lb. Chocolate	good butter
½ cwt. Best White Biscuit	2 well-cured Hams

Who wouldn't have liked Ben Franklin? Braddock admired him. He thought the amazing Philadelphian and George Washington were the two most outstanding Americans he had met.

George Washington was helping with recruiting, but there were dozens of other problems Braddock had to solve. Some of the British officers thought that perhaps they could not be solved. For instance, they believed American officers incompetent. In addition, Quakers vowed they would not defend their homes.

When recruits finally dribbled in, they were slow to catch on to military customs. Some deserted, and when they were overtaken and hauled back to camp, a cat-o'-nine tails lashed their backs. Braddock warned his soldiers he would hang deserters.

His preparations were curious. They indicate that Braddock was alert to his new surroundings and problems. Because of summer days coming up, he ordered an animal's bladder or a piece of leather for each man, cut to the proper size, to be placed inside his hat as protection against the heat—an idea from the plains of India. He knew the march would be hard, and ordered excess equipment discarded. Privates turned in their swords. Officers and sergeants gave up their spontoons (short pikes) and halberds (long-handled spears with hatchet device).

New problems arose. The wagons from England had shafts too wide for the smaller American horse. Governor Dinwiddie had promised that 1,500 packhorses and four hundred Indians would join the British on the march. This called for packers, skilled men who could lash a pack on a horse's back so it would not slide off. And who, outside of a very few frontiersmen, knew how to lead Indians? Even the outstanding American leader, George Washington, had arrived at the stage where he was willing to admit that he did not know how to motivate Indians and make them eager to carry out missions. But in spite of all the difficulties the conglomerate "army" was strengthened by a tough strand: Edward Braddock's will.

Even so, the governor's son, William Shirley, who, like Washington, was an aide, was not sure the formal and regulation-bound General Braddock was the man for the job.

Although problems kept cropping up, Braddock decided he could wait no longer. There was the threat of French reinforcements that might arrive at Fort Duquesne. So, after Easter services on April 10, 1775, Braddock ordered a drummer to beat a snappy signal named "To the General." At this rattling beat, all the tents in camp went down like ninepins. They were folded and packed in the wagons, and the long trek started. In spite of Braddock's preparations, each soldier was burdened with food for eight days, a blanket, his personal articles, an extra pair of shoes, bullets, powder horn, and a musket of approximately nine pounds. Fortunately, the weather was cool.

Braddock was commanding 1,400 regulars, only 260 colonials, and 30 sailors. A few wives marched along— additional mouths that had to be fed. The march started from Alexandria, Virginia, 250 rugged miles stretching ahead to the target.

Up front walked a small screen of guides and surveyors, followed by an advance guard of picked grenadiers and Virginia light horsemen. Next, 300 axmen worked to cut down trees to make a "road." Braddock's coach bumped along over the low-lying stumps as if at any moment it might lose an axle. Farther back, sailors, with their trousers rolled up as if they were swabbing decks, toiled with block and tackle to help the straining horses haul the cannon.

When Braddock's force struggled over a series of Allegheny ridges known as the Devil's Backbone, even the smallest cannon looked like a siege gun. It required tremendous energy to move the heavier cannon that had been taken from the warships. Some days the column advanced only two miles. This worried Braddock because he could not haul enough food to support his men moving at such a slow rate.

Governor Dinwiddie had promised five hundred head of cattle would be delivered on the trail in June, with more to come in August, but where was Dinwiddie's supply officer, who would bring in the herd? General Braddock was not trained to quit. He pressed his command on, more irritable each day over numerous obstacles.

He rightly suspected the French and Indians were well aware he was on the way.

CHAPTER 8

BULLETS AND BRADDOCK

THE advance-guard commander sent General Braddock the message by runner, "Fort Cumberland one-half mile ahead." Braddock leaned out of the window of his coach and said to the sergeant commanding his fifers and drummers, "Strike up something lively."

The musicians responded with "Grenadiers March," the shrill notes of the fifes and the dull thumps of the drums echoing through the woods against the hills.

The long column crawled toward the outpost. It looked like an oversized pigpen, but it meant much to Braddock. It was here that hard work had placed stores for his command. The red, white, and blue of the Union Jack, curling around the pole above the palisades of the fort, signified that the British government was keenly interested in this place at the junction of Wills Creek and the Potomac River (present site of Cumberland, Maryland).

Approximately one hundred ragged Indians, including women and children, hovered about watching the Redcoats and Americans pitch camp. Braddock felt disappointed. Were these the fierce warriors who Dinwiddie said would help him defeat the French? The governor had promised four hundred. Where were the rest?

When the general spoke to the Indians, the Irish-American George Croghan, a trader who himself had once presented a French scalp, acted as interpreter. Braddock talked loftily. Presents, he said, were back in the supply wagons and would be handed out shortly. The great English King, across the water, loved his Indians and was happy they would help defeat the evil French. There *had been* misunderstandings, but all the troubles of the past were buried under the huge mountain north of the fort.

Braddock finished by saying he was grateful for wampum the Indians had given him and that he would pay £5 for scalps. (Both sides had been paying bounties for scalps for years.) He would give £200 for the scalp of the Delaware Chief Wild Cat, and if anyone should be so fortunate as to bring in the hair of Abbé Le Loutre, he would be £100 richer. Then Braddock ordered a salute fired by a few of the cannons to impress the Indians.

The Indians, however, were almost phlegmatic. In addition, George Croghan said they had incredible ideas and beliefs. For example, Andrew Mountour, the half-breed, had been taught by the French that Christ was a Frenchman who had been crucified by the English.

Mishaps began to plague Braddock's army. Hot weather,

thunderstorms, and mosquitoes made life miserable. Much
of the beef in the casks at Fort Cumberland had been im-
properly salted, smelled bad, and was dangerous to eat.
Gambling and drunkenness increased and caused trouble.
Some of the soldiers and Indian girls disappeared in the
woods. So did the horses.

Braddock made a decision. He said that women and children could not accompany the march any farther. This
angered the Indians, and most of them left. They were
using Braddock's order as an excuse, for Indians never
took squaws on war parties.

Many of the officers became disgruntled at the savages'
departure, but few in the force knew how to lead them.
Croghan had lived with Indians, but he was not a leader
and had a bad reputation as a trader because he had cheated
many of them.

Illness overtook one of Braddock's best leaders, George
Washington. He had been sent back to Hampton, Virginia, to obtain £4,000 because the colonials were charging amazing prices for everything—and often not de-
livering. Many of the horses limping into camp were in
poor condition, and some of the wagons wobbling in
were wrecks. Washington's illness was a blow to Braddock, but with the tenacity that was a George Washington hallmark, the Virginian carried out his assignment,
using a wagon as a combination ambulance and hospital.
He was not quitting.

Wagons rounded up by Benjamin Franklin—in far better condition than the others—rolled into camp, but
when the packhorses plodded in, they numbered only
five hundred. Where were the 1,500 promised by Dinwid-

die? Some of the pack animals would have to be used to pull the wagons. Many of the draft horses were exhausted.

Worse news arrived. A Delaware Indian reported to Braddock that he had been in Fort Duquesne the week before and had learned the French expected nine hundred reinforcements. General Braddock reacted in typical Coldstream Guard fashion. He ordered, "Break camp at once. Resume the hike!"

He sent his coach back to Virginia and climbed into the saddle. With his fat stomach pressed against the pommel, he looked his age. But he felt he had a better grip on the command from the back of a horse. One hundred and ten miles to go. Anything could happen, and Edward Braddock knew it.

Braddock kept a tight, all-around security on the march and at the halts. Indians could not break it. They reported to the French in Duquesne, "Braddock never sleeps."

His advance guard marched into a thick, gloomy forest known as the Shades of Death. Again the work of the woodchoppers set the pace. The hike progressed in accordion fashion. The soldiers felt they were forever removing their packs while waiting for the axmen to cut a road, then putting their equipment back on, marching a few hundred yards, sitting down again, then beginning all over again. It was exhausting.

Both colonials and British were awed by the extraordinarily thick and dark woods. Colonials told such wild tales about Indians that they frightened some of the British. Horrid signs appeared on the sides of the trail. French and Indians had blazed trees and tacked scalps to spots where the bark had been hacked away. The grim hanks of hair seemed to warn, "Turn back! You keep on this route, and *your* hair will be the next trophy."

Three stragglers were quickly and brutally murdered. When a combat patrol lashed out in revenge, it killed, by accident, one of the few friendly Indians. Braddock apologized to the dead man's father and ordered an impressive military funeral.

A few days closer to Fort Duquesne, a Redcoat messenger lifted the rear canvas flap of the wagon Washington was riding in. "Beg pardon, sir," the soldier said. "The general presents his compliments and hopes you're well enough to join him up front. He's about four miles ahead."

What was up? Was an Indian attack near? Washington had given his ideas to Braddock—such as they were—on how Indians fought and the best way to stave them off, but the general had been unimpressed. As for the French, the general said loftily, "They're not great fighters."

Washington, in pain and feeling weak, found the general in conference with his top officers. Braddock spoke of his concern over the move the French were making to reinforce Fort Duquesne. "Very logical," Braddock observed. He asked what course was best—keep plugging along like an inchworm or send a fast-moving unit ahead to capture the fort as soon as possible?

Washington said he believed the daring idea would succeed. He wrote later: "I urged it in the warmest possible terms I was master of. . . ."

The next day Washington was sicker. Although a doctor warned he should remain quiet and that overexertion might endanger his life, Washington made arrangements to accompany the approximately 1,400 men and a few 6-

pounders that would knife ahead. Lieutenant Colonel
Thomas Gage (who would become famous as a general
in the American Revolution) commanded the advance
guard. He was a member of a noble family, but unfortunately for the men who served with him he was slow-
thinking and weak.

Colonel Thomas Dunbar would follow the main body
at a slower rate with the wagons and heavier guns. But
in this new, hasty advance, Braddock did not keep up the
careful security measures that had baffled the Indians and,
in turn, the French.

There was excitement at Fort Duquesne as reports
filtered in to Captain Claude de Contrecoeur about the
progress of Braddock's march. The French leader decided wisely to stop work on strengthening the fort and
not wait to be attacked. The fact that his Indians were not
disciplined for a last-ditch defense influenced him.

Captain de Contrecoeur placed Captain Daniel de Beaujeu in command of an attacking force. On the morning of
July 9, 1755, 200 Canadian regulars—dressed like Indians—
and about 650 Hurons, Delawares, Shawnees, and other
tribesmen started out. They anticipated ambush, scalps,
and booty.

But it was not an ambush. About eight miles below the
fort, at two in the afternoon, Beaujeu's attackers col-
lided head-on with Braddock's scouts. Both sides were
surprised.

Captain Beaujeu fell, a bullet through his brain. Some of
his attackers turned tail and ran back toward their fort.
The Redcoat Lieutenant Colonel Gage, reacting like a
tortoise, failed to follow up this sudden advantage. Ad-

vancing to his support, the main column jammed up in the narrow clearing. Musket balls whiz-cracked through the forest. Indians from Canada howled like devils fresh out of hell. They needed no commands. They scattered quickly, hid behind bushes and trees, and fired into both sides of Braddock's long column. In the noise, excitement, and confusion, the British officers did not react in orthodox manner; they neglected to seize the high ground to the right of the trail. Their soldiers were not worrying about tactics, but tried to pick up the enemy in the sights of their muskets while they shouted as a battle cry, "Long live the King."

A handful of British ran to the rear along the road. Men fighting up front were concerned when they learned this. A rumor spread that French and Indians were attacking the wagon train. More soldiers of the King and colonials rushed back. Attackers picked them off as if they were in a shooting gallery.

Braddock was furious. He galloped wildly about, laying on some of the fear-crazed men with the flat of his sword. Washington, still weak but buoyed by the excitement, rode toward the danger to try to find company officers to make them control their men.

General Braddock's horse was shot. He jumped up, took another horse from an orderly, and continued to try to control the battle. This scene was repeated four more times. Washington himself lost two horses while he was in the saddle. He asked Braddock for attack orders, but the general shook his head: "No!"

A bullet found Braddock. He tumbled from his horse, badly wounded in the arm and side. Gage, advance guard commander, had vanished. (Later, after the fight ended, he was found with a small, rallied detachment behind the rear guard.)

The French controlled the battlefield. They picked up Braddock's official papers, including his plans for over-all strategy, as well as Major Stobo's sketch of Fort Duquesne. (It was this that almost placed Stobo's head on the block.)

As the horrible scene quieted, the battle excitement left Washington and was replaced with extreme fatigue. However, he rustled up a wagon to carry the dying general. No one formed a rear guard.

Braddock's defeat was total. Death overtook him as his entire force reeled back. When the question of burial arose, Washington suggested a grave be dug in the middle of the road about one mile from the ruins of Fort Necessity so Indians could not find it and desecrate the body. George Washington read the burial service. The retreat continued. Braddock's grave was hidden by the ruts the wagon wheels made as they churned and creaked back to civilization.

Washington now assumed command at Fort Cumberland.

Colonel Thomas Dunbar, who had crossed the seas to fight under Braddock, was badly frightened. It would have taken a rare commander to have led a counterattack not knowing the strength of the enemy.

In this crisis, Dunbar thought only of getting away. He spiked his cannon by hammering nails in the touchholes, burned other supplies, including the hard-to-get wagons, dumped powder into the streams, and led fifteen hundred soldiers on a fast march back to Philadelphia. His retreat alarmed the colonists almost as much as Edward Braddock's defeat. Then Colonel Dunbar said he might go into winter quarters—in July! He soon marched his command all the way to Albany, New York.

Braddock, on his fateful trek, had employed every precaution except distant patrols to scout the enemy. His defeat was such a shock to Britons and Americans that for over a hundred years their writers damned him. It became fashionable to adopt the "Braddock myth": that victory had not been gained by the prowess of the enemy, but because he was incompetent.

Braddock was not a bad commander. He was, in reality, a brave and determined general, who tried to carry out a difficult, unnecessary mission. It was a task not well thought out by political and military leaders an ocean away—men who had only foggy ideas about the situation in America.

CHAPTER 9

HOW BENJAMIN FRANKLIN
BECAME A GENERAL

THE frontier trembled. It seemed incredible that a
British major general, with two regiments of Redcoats reinforced by American volunteers, could be defeated by Frenchmen and Indians. It was also unbelievable
that a British colonel would hurry his command away from
danger.

Thousands of settlers from little farms dotting the
western frontiers of Pennsylvania, Maryland, and Virginia
fled eastward to escape the torch and tomahawk. Those
who remained, or who did not move fast enough, saw
loved ones killed, women and children dragged away to
captivity. The Indian raiders moved in small bands to
spread their own particular type of hell, which included
burning homes and barns and driving away livestock.

Only tiny Fort Cumberland protected Virginia and Pennsylvania, and it was simple to bypass it.

Terrifying rumors were whispered, such as that the French now had a series of forts stretching almost three thousand miles from the St. Lawrence, down the Ohio, along the Mississippi to its outlet in the Gulf of Mexico.

One of the results of the extraordinary defeat was restlessness among Negro slaves. Dinwiddie wrote: "They have been very audacious on the Defeat on the Ohio. These poor creatures imagine the Fr. will give them their freedom. . . ."

Dinwiddie and the citizens of Virginia were fortunate in having George Washington as a military leader. He rode into Winchester to find hundreds of frightened refugees, and informed Dinwiddie that the Blue Ridge was now Virginia's frontier. For the next few years Washington slaved, in his determined, conscientious way, to make the northwestern part of Virginia safe from Indian raids. At times he led fewer than a hundred men, and what made matters extremely trying was that these usually were miserable, undisciplined individuals. As far as Washington's future was concerned, the war was a furnace tempering him with knowledge and toughness for the greater fight yet to come.

The situation in Pennsylvania was just as chaotic as in Virginia. Pennsylvania's governor and other political leaders received floods of petitions signed by frontiersmen begging for help. Americans had not seen Indian raids on such a scale for a generation, and previous French and Indian wars had never lashed Pennsylvania, Maryland, or Virginia.

In mid-October, 1755, the Delawares swooped down on Penn's Creek settlement, only 140 miles from Philadelphia, killing or capturing twenty-five persons. In November, the tide swept even closer to the principal Pennsylvania city. Raiding parties of Indians terrified settlers in Berks and Northampton counties, roughly fifty miles from the capital. The Shawnees attacked German settlers in the Lehigh Mountains.

Into Philadelphia, in November, marched five hundred to a thousand German farmers with ghastly souvenirs in their wagons: the corpses of dear friends and relatives who had been scalped and murdered. They placed them on the steps of the capitol.

Church bells tolled in the city at the slightest alarm.

There was almost a civil war. The Quakers said it was a sin to fight, that they would not fight to protect their homes and would not be taxed for a war. Another faction strongly resented this. The situation was so upsetting that Governor Robert Hunter Morris of Pennsylvania sent for a man he feared politically and asked him to secure the frontier northwest of Philadelphia. This is how Benjamin Franklin became a "general."

As soon as he could, the portly Franklin mounted a warhorse and rode out of the capital, wearing epaulets, with a sword hanging at his belt. Clattering along with him trotted a company of cavalry as protection. On the road to danger, he met refugees streaming toward the city. The frightened people warned him, but he trotted on to the present Reading–Allentown–Bethlehem–Easton area, roughly forty miles from Philadelphia.

Franklin knew little of army regulations. In this emergency, he depended upon his famous common sense. He built a series of crude forts from which his militia could strike Indian raiders. He worked hard for six weeks, and took time to train his volunteers to carry out orders. When he was satisfied the line was secure, "General" Franklin, as his men called him, left the forts and rode back to the even rougher ground of colonial politics.

There was also trouble to the north, because Braddock's defeat had changed Indian ideas. To many tribes, the British effort now had the odor of a losing cause. William Johnson worked long hours to keep the Iroquois on the side of the British. But the Indians saw that the colonies remained disunited and argumentative. The Iroquois themselves were split, although many Mohawks still favored Britain. Then when the Indians learned Governor Shirley was working on a foray up the Atlantic coast, they thought he was moving in the wrong direction.

CHAPTER 10

EXILE OF THE ACADIANS

THE strike against Nova Scotia was risky. It involved an overwater expedition, and it was barging into an already very troubled area. But in 1755, Governor Shirley was busy planning it; this was one of the three expeditions Braddock had approved at Annapolis. For years, the British government had known it would have to face the turbulent situation in Nova Scotia, and it now thought action could be put off no longer.

Affairs in Nova Scotia were in disorder. Britain firmly believed it owned the land, yet the French lilies flew over two forts, in addition to Louisbourg. Boundaries were as vague as writing on water. Most of the thirteen thousand Acadians were Catholic peasants, farmers who lived in fear of the warlike priest Abbé Le Loutre. To add to the smoke, for forty years Acadians had been living under protection of the British flag, yet they were loyal to an enemy nation; most Acadians thought of themselves as French.

The Abbé Le Loutre brought fire into the ferment by carrying out orders from France. He spread the word among the Acadians that the British were their deadly enemies, and he let it be known that, if they failed to help the French, he would send Indians, whom he controlled, to raid their farms.

The British had been pressing for several years to have the Acadians take a loyalty oath to the Crown. Le Loutre warned the ignorant people that, if they submitted to this, they would be denied the sacraments of the Church and would be headed for hell. Consequently, the pious Acadians were caught between two dangers.

The Acadians irritated both nations. In spite of the Abbé Le Loutre and his threats, most of them said they would not help France—nor would they take the British oath.

Rumors and false promises had spread like a plague over the land for years, the Acadian grapevine whispering that the British would deport those who failed to take the oath. Eight years before, in 1747, Governor Shirley had assured the Acadians that this was false; a proclamation by King George II the next year said the same thing.

In 1749 a log had been thrown on the smoldering fire when a convoy of British ships landed 2,500 British colonists on the site of modern Halifax. Another stick in the blaze was the Micmac Indian tribe, who demanded that Britain give them all of Nova Scotia.

Violence spread over the lonely countryside as Indians ambushed small groups of English settlers and when Louisbourg authorities began to pay for British scalps.

The situation was so upsetting that the British governor wrote to the colonies for help. Consequently, tough New England rangers under Major Joseph Gorham were ordered to Nova Scotia.

Gorham's rangers filtered through the woods and worked their armed sloops along the rocky coasts. His rangers were something new in American warfare—men who could outwit Indians and rush a French outpost like the specially selected and carefully trained grenadiers.

Violence begat violence. Not only were British scalps bringing money in Louisbourg, but Gorham's rangers were rewarded with £10 for Indian scalps in Halifax. Once in a while they brought in a blond-haired scalp and received money. Life in Acadia began to resemble the hell Abbé Le Loutre preached about.

Colonel Charles Lawrence, British governor of Acadia, had long been convinced that settling the question of the oath of allegiance was the prime step toward peace. Governor Lawrence's idea coincided with plans in London and in the conference at Annapolis.

In May, 1755, Shirley sent thirty-seven ships carrying 2,000 volunteers and 250 Redcoats to Nova Scotia. The garrison at Fort Beauséjour (150 French soldiers and, surprisingly, 240 Acadians) surrendered after a little fighting—in spite of vigorous protests from the warlike Abbé. He escaped before the French lilies were hauled down. Next, the British captured Fort St. John.

Lawrence now consulted his council and two British

admirals. "What to do?" was the question. The British believed the Acadians to be treacherous and unreliable. They said the Acadians had not been honest and had aided the enemy. Consequently, the British set fire to Acadian homes and barns and seized Acadian cattle. Almost seven thousand of the wretched, half-starved people were handled brutally as they were hustled aboard British ships, to be put ashore along the coasts of the colonies.

Those who escaped ran for cover like animals before a hunter. About two thousand Acadians reached other parts of Canada, only to be mistreated. Some eventually traveled to France, where they were ill repaid for their loyalty by the French government. Numbers sailed to Louisiana, where their descendants—the Acadians, corrupted to "Cajuns"—are living today. A few paid their way to the West Indies. The hapless people received the best treatment in Massachusetts, Connecticut, Pennsylvania, Maryland, and in New Orleans. The harsh expulsions went on for seven years.

Longfellow's poem "Evangeline" ("This is the forest primeval . . ."), written almost a century after the expulsions, focused attention on the Acadians in a way that only a poem can. Longfellow chose, however, not to picture the crosscurrents, faithlessness, and politics behind the uprooting of the Acadians. He wrote near the end of this long poem, "Some wandered back to their native land to die in its bosom." These few took the oath so they could farm again on the lonely land.

Just before the expulsions began, the French managed to slip sixty-eight companies of soldiers into Louisbourg under the nose of a British blockading fleet. This was an especially skillful exploit because King Louis XV had let the French Navy run down.

Britain's command of the seas was a tremendous factor in her favor. It let her send soldiers and supplies anywhere on the globe, and it kept the French from shipping reinforcements to America and India. Canada could not raise enough food to feed its own population and also the French soldiers in Canada. With British warships lying off French seaports and the mouth of the St. Lawrence River, as well as scouring the seas, very little food got through. It became difficult for the French even to secure sufficient presents with which to maintain the loyalty of their Indian allies.

One incident highlights the indecisive attitude of French seamen.

Captain Richard Howe sailed a British man-of-war close to the French warship *Alicide*.

The French skipper shouted across the water, "Are we at peace or war?"

"At peace, at peace!" Howe called back. Then he opened fire. The French warship *Lys* was also raked in the surprise cannonade. Three hundred and thirty French sailors became prisoners.

Later in the fall, the British captured 300 French merchant vessels and about 6,000 sailors.

The French king, Louis XV, refused to declare war. He enjoyed his rosy dreams. He thought he could have things his own way: continue his thrusts against the American colonies, enduring British "piracy," as he called it, and not bring on war between the two nations.

CHAPTER II

CONFLICTS AND CHAOS IN ALBANY

I N 1755, the arc of the frontier extended a scant fifteen
miles northwest of Albany, New York, and four times
that distance through the woods to Lac Saint Sacrement
(later Lake George). Beyond lay beaver country and the
aggressive French with their Indian allies, many of the
latter still at a very primitive level of civilization.

The fortified town of Albany had never been a monot-
onous place. This gateway to the west, an important fur-
trading post, had seen exciting and bitter times since its
earliest days. It had witnessed results of cruelties inflicted
by the Indians, including the devilish work of the Mohawks on Father Jogues. Townspeople had seen the devas-
tations caused by intertribal wars. They had seen the
Mohawks fight the Mohegans, and massacres of Mohawks
by Abnaki warriors.

87

In Albany, a town of three thousand, Dutch traders competed against each other and against British traders for furs. Back in 1652, terror had raged when soldiers from the miserable little Dutch Fort Orange oppressed the settlers. Albany had also witnessed religious intolerance toward Lutheran citizens by officials of the West India Company, when followers of Martin Luther had held their own religious services and had sung hymns.

The village had seen the takeover of the Dutch fort by the British, who renamed it Fort Albany. However, the principal factor keeping the town in a fever of excitement was its location. Albany, almost in the zone of close combat, could document hostilities with French and Indians for over half a century.

A ten-foot palisade in 1755 all but hid the bastions of the old log-and-earth fort. A few spires, the highest the tower of the Dutch Reformed Church, dominated the landscape and gave the village a look of importance. Smoke drifting over the trees from the nearby forest and the sound of the ax testified that the work of clearing land was still under way. A stone wall, pitted with loopholes for muskets, stretched from the north gate to the Hudson River. About nine small docks and landing places bordered the waterfront. In the river, sloops and three-masted ships lay at anchor. Sharp-pointed, flat-bottomed bateaux and canoes, necessary adjuncts of the fur and fish trade, dotted the wide stream.

In the summer, the turmoil reached even larger proportions because Albany was the base for two military campaigns. About three thousand colonial militia had pitched their tents or were living in log cabins on nearby flats (probably on the site of modern Rensselaer). When off duty, the soldiers sprawled on neat benches under rows of button trees in front of the one- and two-story houses of Albany, most of them brick. The soldiers ogled industrious housewives who wore short skirts which showed their ankles, and high heels, and bodices with sleeves that were wide above the elbows.

Occasionally down the wide main street clattered a horse hauling a wagon driven by a slave, or by a Dutch, German, or British settler. Horses and wagons were needed for the campaign to the north, but as Braddock had found, they were hard to hire. There had long been a saying in Albany: "A Dutchman loves his horse more than his wife."

The two campaigns against the French and Indians—one to the north, the other to the west—were practically in opposition. The greatest scramble between British generals was for friendly Indians to carry the war to the enemy. Strong crosscurrents of jealousy existed between the two leaders, Governor Shirley and William Johnson, illustrating only too well the ancient German proverb, "Jealousy does more harm than witchcraft."

The seeds of the trouble had been sown when General Braddock decided two campaigns would be based at Albany.

Shirley, who had become commander in chief on Braddock's death, was anxious to start his strike west against the French fort at Niagara. This vigorous governor made the bad error of allowing his ambition to control his sense. Shirley burned with desire to etch his name in history. To ensure this, he thought he had to enlist as many Iroquois as he could. He was commander in chief, yet he was so eager for glory he cared nothing about how many Indians helped Johnson. Shirley also had a technical problem bothering him: how to govern Massachusetts from a campfire along the Mohawk.

Shirley sent agents among the Iroquois. His men told the Indians it was wise to accompany Shirley on his westward smash. The agents gave the Indians rum as a bribe, and the Indians got drunk. When the Indians recovered, they listened to the agent's harsh song: "William Johnson is not to be trusted. He lacks Governor Shirley's tremendous authority. It is best to GO WITH SHIRLEY!" The Mohawks wasted no time reporting this to Johnson, and the jealousy between the two leaders became laced with hatred.

Johnson did talk to Shirley, to try to straighten out the chaos, but accomplished nothing. Shirley, far from tactful and not a broad thinker, was kindling fires with which he would have to contend in the future.

The jealousy grew and almost wrecked the plans. In addition, Lieutenant Governor DeLancey entered the picture, as he resented Shirley's consuming desire for power and glory. The New Yorker could not stomach sitting on the sidelines while two expeditions readied themselves in Albany, and instead of trying to help Shirley, DeLancey wrote letters to powerful friends in London to undermine the Massachusetts governor.

At the same time, an adventurer from Great Britain, Thomas Pownall, worked to oust Shirley as governor. Pownall not only wanted Shirley replaced but saw himself as governor. Johnson, too, was taking up his quill to dig Shirley's political grave by sending letters across the Atlantic bearing the theme song "Shirley's conduct not only shakes the system of Indian affairs but gives me fresh anxieties and expenses." A sinkhole of backstairs craftiness existed.

To thicken the intrigue, Shirley descended to the same level by secretly writing to leaders in London of his difficulties with Johnson.

During preparations for the campaigns, Johnson held a ten-day conference with Iroquois chiefs in his fortress-like home on the Mohawk, forty miles west of Albany. He daubed scarlet paint on his face, donned Indian ceremonial headdress, and yelled and danced with the Indians. Johnson understood the Iroquois, respected their customs, and dealt with them in their own terms. No wonder they loved him. He was a remarkable man with Indians.

But he began to show the strain. Although he was a most successful trader, he no doubt felt deficient in the hard job of organizing an army. Men he would lead, from Connecticut, Rhode Island, New Hampshire, and New York—numbering about 3,500—were the rawest kind of soldiers. Many were fresh from trades or small businesses. Some sported militia uniforms faced with red. Others wore rough work clothes with breeches thrust into thigh-high gaiters buttoning on the side. They carried several makes of muskets, few of which could be fitted with bayonets. They relied on tomahawks and hatchets for close combat.

To train his militia and to try to instill discipline, General Johnson ordered maneuvers on the flats. Iroquois families watched while the braves, with their faces painted, played war against the whites. Little was accomplished. The white men tired fast and complained to Johnson that they had come to fight the enemy.

Although Johnson allowed himself to be swamped with

other details to get ready to fight, such as how to obtain, store, and transport food, how to procure horses and wagons, how to move artillery and its heavy ammunition, he found time to endorse:

SOME HINTS FOR A COMMANDING OFFICER

If you loose dont despair.

Let nothing ruffle your Temper, be always cool, happen what will.

You may have occasion for Irons for some sort of prisoners.

. . . each [sentry] to have a watchfull Dog, and supported by out Guards.

A General officer must keep a good Table.

Engage in no Action of importance without a Council of War, and let every one's opinion be carefully noted. This will Justify you upon all occasions.

Johnson's staunch belief in a council of war would cause him trouble later on. He was anxious to avoid responsibility for serious decisions. He had a most capable second-in-command in General Phineas Lyman, a Yale graduate, but Johnson could not delegate details to anyone. He wrote:

[My tent is crowded] from morning to night with Indians, with officers, etc., all impatient to be heard, each thinking his own affairs more important than the Others. I am obliged to hear them all. . . . It is miserable.

In midsummer 1755, William Johnson started north through the forest with his army, toward Crown Point on Lake Champlain. A few days later Governor Shirley led his men west along the Mohawk. Shirley felt disappointed because only a few Iroquois had joined him. General Johnson and the scheming DeLancey had seen to this.

Johnson, too, was upset over lack of Iroquois help; only old King Hendrick and fifty Mohawks accompanied him.

Six days later, General Johnson felt slightly better. Two hundred more Indians reported. More would come, they said. But Johnson knew that time and numbers meant little to Indians. They went to war when they felt like it and only for a few months at a time. And no chief could make them go. Eventually, about five hundred Indians joined Johnson.

On the trail north, he received terrible news. Four Mohawk scouts he had sent to Canada walked out of the forest. They said that papers the French had picked up after Braddock's death had enabled them to make new plans. "Coming toward you," the scouts declared, "are eight thousand French soldiers and Indians." It was a report that would have frightened greater leaders than William Johnson.

CHAPTER 12

GALL AT LAKE GEORGE;
TROUBLES AT FORT OSWEGO

B UT JOHNSON had no idea of quitting. He marched on. Cannoneers and horses worked in the heat to tug artillery through the forest, men and animals straining as though, if they pulled but a few more yards, the work would become easy. Swarms of tormenting insects buzzed about them.

Captain William Eyre, artillery commander, used every trick he had learned in the British Army to help move the guns forward. The six tremendous 18-pounders, each weighing almost three tons, and even the smallest cannon and mortars, looked like monsters. These black demons were expected to play the major part in the tremendous mission of overcoming eight thousand French and Indians.

Later, on this hot August day in 1755, General Johnson

and his staff saw a sparkling blue lake through the firs. "Lac Saint Sacrement," an aide said. "One of the prettiest lakes in this country."

Johnson's voice boomed, "The name is hereby changed in honor of His Gracious Majesty to 'Lake George.'" To a secretary he added, "Kindly see this is included in my next report to His Majesty's ministers." William Johnson seldom overlooked an opportunity to advance himself.

At noon, cooks spread a white cloth on the brown pine needles for Johnson and his senior officers. From the hampers came smoked venison, smoked ham, peas, hard rolls, lemon punch, and wedges of Stilton cheese, which Johnson anointed with port wine. The men at the trailside picnic did not appear like soldiers about to confront an enemy army of eight thousand or more.

In spite of the peril, life under General Johnson seemed pleasant, because he rarely gave an order unless it was first discussed in council. He liked presiding where each

"Sir William Johnson."
Oil on canvas by
John Wollaston.
*Courtesy Collection Albany
Institute of History and Art*

senior officer had his say. Majority rule was his idea. His top officers approved because this gave them a voice in the campaign. Few were experienced enough to know Johnson's system would not work under battle pressures.

At the southern end of Lake George, the officers voted to have trees cut so camp could be pitched and a fort built. Johnson, who liked naming places, announced, "Eventually this will be Fort William Henry." Farther back, at the bend of the Hudson where the artillery had been landed, he had named the place where another defensive work would be constructed Fort Edward, in honor of one of the King's grandsons. The forest rang at both places with the noise of hard labor. Johnson split his army between the two locations.

There was more bad news for Johnson at Lake George. Some of the Mohawk scouts announced they were leaving. "We will be back," they promised. But Johnson never saw them again at the lake.

The scouts may have had the word that a clash was near. On September 1, came Baron Von Dieskau hunting for Englishmen. With him walked French soldiers, Canadian militia, and about 600 Indians. His force totaled 3,200, not the 8,000 that had been reported. But General Von Dieskau had his troubles; he was not used to such untrained soldiers as the Canadians and their Indians. He split his force, bringing only 1,500 to the attack.

When General Johnson received news of Von Dieskau's advance, he assembled a council of war. The council voted to send about one thousand soldiers and a few Iroquois against the French. Old Mohawk Chief Hendrick, one of the wisest at the council, warned Johnson, "The force you are sending is too small to be of great use, too large to sacrifice." But Johnson was an odd commanding officer: he felt that he had but one vote in the council. He was not going to change its decision.

Chief Hendrick bravely rode his pony through the woods with the weak thrust. Shortly, when enemy muskets and war whoops resounded through the forest from an ambush, Hendrick fell from his animal, dead.

Colonel Ephraim Williams, leader of the foray, climbed a rock so he could direct his men. A musket ball smashed into his brain. As soon as the Indians saw King Hendrick and Williams fall, they turned and ran. *Being* ambushed was not their kind of fighting. Most of Johnson's men saved themselves by rushing back to the partially finished fort at Lake George.

On came General Von Dieskau. When he arrived, he discovered Johnson's men barricaded behind wagons lying on their sides, felled trees, and bateaux. Eyre's artillery held the center. Von Dieskau looked over the situation with a trained eye and ordered a charge. His Indian allies viewed this with horror. They much preferred bushwhacking. They turned and ran into the forest, many of the partially trained Canadians with them. Von Dieskau's crippled force charged and suffered heavy casualties.

Both Von Dieskau and Johnson were wounded.

Thanks to General Phineas Lyman, Johnson's force held. Von Dieskau was captured. When the badly shaken French leader was carried to Johnson's tent, he was followed by a pack of Indians, who circled about, howling like angry wolves.

"What are they after?" the baron asked Johnson.

"You," Johnson replied. "They want to cut you up in little pieces and smoke you in their pipes. With me you are safe."

The French reeled back through the forest to Fort St. Frédéric (Crown Point). Johnson's council of war voted not to follow them, although this was vital to success. The French pulled back only thirty-five miles from the scene of the battle.

Johnson now wrote glowing reports of the battle to London, where he was hailed as "Our Only Hero." Parliament was so delighted with the battle it voted him £5,000, and the King made him a baronet. General Phineas Lyman, the real hero of the fight, was not mentioned and received nothing. Johnson glossed over his failure to take Crown Point, nor did he write that soon after the battle he was having difficulty controlling his men.

Johnson needed to know what the French were doing, so he turned to a company of woodsmen from New Hampshire whom Governor Shirley had formed as rangers. The natural leader of the group was Robert Rogers, an ambitious, fearless husky, six feet tall and powerful. He loved danger and hated paper work. When Rogers led four selected rangers into enemy country toward the French Fort St. Frédéric at Crown Point, Lake Champlain, at Johnson's order, he was taking his life in his hands. No one knew if they would ever be seen again.

At the time, the rangers lacked uniforms. Rogers himself wore a linen shirt, a breech clout in place of breeches, and Indian-style leggings that came halfway up the thigh. All avoided buckskin. It was too hot for summer, and when the rain came, it shrank and felt uncomfortably clammy.

Rogers' small patrol paddled a bateau quietly on Lake George by night, hiding the craft and themselves by day. One careless slip meant death.

Insects bored into them. Rogers wrote later, "The Natts and Musketoes bothered us." For two and a half days Rogers and his rangers scouted activities in the fort and in the surrounding country. When they returned and reported to Johnson, they were heroes. Johnson was not a bit sure he liked Rogers' skyrocketing to fame, but he gave him a few days' rest and sent him back into enemy territory.

This time the rangers paddled a birchbark canoe at night north on the lovely lake. Rogers left the canoe, and three men to watch it, in the woods near the end of the lake and scouted ahead with one man. They got the information they were after, but before they returned to Johnson, all of Rogers' patrol fought Indians.

"We found about a thousand Frenchmen campin' on the west side of Lake Champlain at Ti," Rogers reported to Johnson. "And they had a fort, a grand encampment, holding about three thousand more." This was strategic Ticonderoga, between Lake George and Lake Champlain. After exaggerated news from the Indians, Rogers' report was a relief.

After this, when icy rains came in late November, Johnson left men to garrison Fort Edward and Fort William Henry and pulled back to the comforts of Albany with most of his force. His hip was bothering him, and no doubt he realized he was a better trader than a general. For a while, Johnson would play a more minor role in the war.

Johnson's failure to push on and beat the French at

Lake George, while disguised as a tremendous victory, did
not deceive the Iroquois. True, he had pushed the northern
New York frontier fifty miles closer to Canada, but what
was fifty miles? The loss of Chief Hendrick brought many
Indians to hard realities. They decided quietly to favor
the French—until it looked as if the British might win—
and to spy for both sides—for a price.

While Johnson was failing in his mission, Governor
Shirley, who had been commissioned a major general, was
having his troubles.

Insufficient shipping on the Mohawk and summer
storms had delayed him in his goal of capturing Fort
Niagara, via Fort Oswego. And his force of fifteen hundred men had help from only a few Indians. Then when
his expedition arrived at the Great Carrying Place—the
four-mile portage from the Mohawk River to Lake Oneida
(near present-day Rome, New York), backbreaking labor
began.

The portage trail was rough. In order to transport guns,
cannonballs, powder, food, bateaux, and other articles
over the carry, the men had to walk the four miles over
and over again. On half of the trips they served as beasts
of burden. Men Shirley had brought along to paddle his
bateaux and workmen crowned his troubles by deserting.

While his men were sweating on the portage trail, Shirley wrote to one of King George's Secretaries of State:

[To] gain Intelligence of the Strength and Circum-
stances of the French at Niagara, I have employ'd two
trusty intelligent Indians, and two Albany Traders who

are to accompany them in Indian Disguise, all extremely well qualify'd. . . .

From my Intelligence of the Strength of the French at Niagara, it should appear a rash Proceeding for me to attempt the Reduction of the Fort there this Season with the Forces I have with me. It might result not only loss of the Troops but of Oswego itself.

When Shirley and his men arrived at Fort Oswego at the end of four hard weeks (it took the provisions longer), an impressive officer welcomed him. Shirley was glad to shake hands with Captain John Bradstreet, who, back in 1745, had helped convince him Louisbourg could be captured.

Bradstreet, a Redcoat with a burly build, strong-featured and with graying hair, was as rugged as he looked. He was one of the few British officers for whom Americans relished working, a dynamic leader caring little for popularity, who concentrated on getting the job done. Bradstreet was a rare individual. Although he was popular with those serving under him, his equals and superiors at times found him very difficult.

When Bradstreet showed Shirley around Oswego, Shirley was amazed to find not a fort but in reality a run-down trading post. He ordered the captain to strengthen it at once. Shirley also had work started on two forts close by, and on another at the Great Carrying Place. He ordered construction of several warships so the British would have control of Lake Ontario. He saw clearly that if he could establish a strong base and a fleet at Oswego, French communications with their trading posts to the west would be cut. If the French could not get trade goods to the western Indians, those tribes would soon abandon them.

This was all fine, but Shirley was on thin ice. Back in Virginia, Braddock had warned him not to spend the government's money unless he had approval from London. Shirley, however, was in no mood to sit still and wait for a sailing vessel to carry a request for funds across the Atlantic and to sail back with the answer. There was work to be done. He salved his conscience with the thought that Oswego was one of the most important areas in North America in the war with the French.

Shirley was doing too much too soon. Not only was he disregarding important orders about funds, but, although honest himself, he was careless with money. He overlooked problems and difficulties, such as the scarcity of boats, wagons, and horses west of the Hudson, and how hard it was to move supplies. In addition, he was often a poor judge of men. Some of the assistants he selected proved to be first-class scoundrels and pocketed the government's money. His enemies had no difficulty in gathering points against him.

However, Shirley saw an important point of strategy. He could not move along Lake Ontario against Fort Niagara because he would risk being cut off by soldiers from Fort Frontenac, fifty miles away.

The small picture was harder to see. Patrols, and the four men he sent out to gain intelligence, returned with conflicting information. It was obvious that both French forts were weak, but there was little Shirley could do. And a report from Red Head, an Onondaga, promptly forwarded to London with other information, had an ominous, thundercloud tone:

Red Head, who says he left Ft. Frontenac about five weeks ago [reports] they expect soon from Canada a much larger Number of Troops, with an officer call'd the General. . . . Then they should make the English a Visit at Oswego and attack it.

The "officer call'd the General" would indeed have impact on the war.

A few days later, Shirley left Oswego for civilization, leaving seven hundred men and Lieutenant Colonel James Mercer to brave the Ontario winter and any French and Indians who might appear. While he was returning on the Mohawk and experimenting with a whaleboat, the craft capsized and William Shirley almost lost his life.

Shirley did, at last, lose his official life. Letters to London from Johnson, DeLancey, and Pownall, undermined him and caused his recall in the following year. When Shirley and Johnson got better acquainted, they became friends of a sort, but the damage to Governor Shirley's official career had occurred.

Shirley was a rare colonial leader, well meaning and energetic, but he seldom thought things through. He could see what needed to be done, but he did not know how to go about it. One of his errors was to compete with William Johnson for Iroquois warriors. When Shirley was recalled to London, he left a bad financial and organizational mess. The British leader who took Shirley's place found the war in a dreadful snarl.

In spite of fighting going on in America and on the high seas, the world war did not start until 1756. Then the fever jumped oceans and spread. "The French and

Indian War," as Americans called it, was known in Europe as the Seven Years' War.

This world war, which lasted from 1756 to 1763, saw France, Austria, Russia, Saxony, Sweden, and (after 1762), Spain fighting England, Prussia, and Hanover. Whatever its name, soldiers and sailors and native tribesmen fought and died in the Philippine Islands, in India and Africa, throughout central Europe, up and down the coasts and rivers of the Western Hemisphere, and across the seven seas. The battles were savage and deadly.

In Europe, Frederick II (Frederick the Great) of Prussia, struggled desperately to hang on to the province of Silesia, which he had taken from Austria in the War of the Austrian Succession. Thanks to English support and his own skill as a general, he barely managed to outlast his enemies. Elsewhere, English fleets and expeditionary forces gradually beat the French and Spaniards in Asia, Africa, and America.

Even with their pressing new involvements all around the world, the British had realized by the end of 1755 that the war in North America needed better generalship. Consequently, an unusual Scot left London for New York.

CHAPTER 13

TATTERED UNION JACK

SHIRLEY's replacement stepped ashore in a style startling to New York City. In mid-July, 1756, the Earl of Loudoun, a Scot named John Campbell, landed—with aides, secretaries, his mistress, coachmen, and more than a dozen servants, while longshoremen handled a shipload of his baggage. The earl also brought along three carriages, nineteen horses, and crates of rare wines.

Word traveled around the city that the man who now had the mission of carrying on the war could be as snappish as a terrier guarding a bone. The Earl of Loudoun took an instant dislike to Governor Shirley and grilled him.

News Loudoun received, as soon as he got his breath, made him surlier. Raiders from Canada had braved the winter to pierce the route between Albany and Fort

Oswego, and after fierce hand-to-hand fighting one of the forts Shirley had erected at the great portage had been burned, blown up, and its garrison slaughtered.

There was a bright spot. Captain John Bradstreet, at Shirley's order, had taken about 700 bateaumen and 300 soldiers and had muscled supplies through the gauntlet to Oswego. The forceful Bradstreet made his men roll barrels of salt pork across twenty-one miles of ice on Lake Oneida. He arrived to find a garrison starving on a ration of two ounces of salt pork and a third of a loaf of bread. With such miserable daily fare, many of the people in the fort were ill.

On the return trip the enemy ambushed him, but he quickly sized up the situation and beat off the raiders, who withdrew.

A serious and weighty question rose out of Bradstreet's victory: What was the best plan?

The Earl of Loudoun did not possess the imagination to be a great commander. This, and an inability to delegate details, handicapped him. He was also hobbled because Shirley's work committed him to Oswego. He could not use his own plan of going for Quebec by way of the St. Lawrence. So he spread his ten thousand men in driblets over the northern landscape. Involvements with trifles also hurt him. Shortly after his arrival he wrote lengthy letters to the King detailing his difficulties with discipline. He even reported what a sergeant was doing.

But Loudoun had his superior points. He was a sound, veteran soldier who could see what had to be done. He expanded the rangers. He improved the British way of fighting in the forest. He also persuaded the colonies, except the southern ones, to cooperate a little better in furnishing men for the war. Not all the seeds Benjamin Franklin had sown were lost.

People in the colonies felt anxious over the fate of Fort Oswego. Who would lead the party to reinforce it? Bradstreet was too junior in rank, and he was up to his scalp lock with the supply problem. So Loudoun chose General Daniel Webb, a recent arrival. Webb's record up until he set foot in America was excellent.

While Webb was on the way up the Mohawk to Oswego with a regiment and boatmen to handle supplies, the situation at Oswego changed. The "man call'd the General" appeared.

Behind the French leader, the Marquis de Montcalm, came French soldiers, dragging eighty cannon, as well as *voyageurs* and Western Indians—Hurons, Ojibwas, Ottawas, Winnebagos, and Miamis.

When Colonel Mercer, the leader at Oswego, saw the French and Indian army and its cannon, he decided to abandon one of the forts and to make his stand in the other two.

Montcalm ordered his artillery into position. His men believed in him, and the Indians called him "a man with the spirit of the eagle." The bombardment began. Cannonballs ripped through the rotten palisade as if it were bread and plowed through makeshift breastworks and barrels of salt pork. The fort sounded as if it were coming apart, and indeed it was. A round shot cut Mercer in two. When he fell, the heart went out of the outgunned defenders. An hour after his death the red, white, and blue Union Jack fluttered down, and a white rag dangled from the flagpole.

Indians dashed in. They found rum, gulped it, and

began to murder and scalp the wounded and other prisoners. Shrieks from about one hundred soldiers' wives, who lived in the fort, seemed only to excite the savages. Horrified, Montcalm finally succeeded in stopping the slaughter by promising them presents.

About seventy-five died in the massacre. The fort was set on fire, its smoke signaling the end of British power on Lake Ontario. *Voyageurs* formed a column on the lake with forty bateaux, and Montcalm boarded one for Montreal. At least fifteen hundred people were going into captivity.

Terrified escapees from Oswego sped down the Mohawk toward Albany. When they met General Webb's relief expedition at the long portage, they told him Montcalm and thousands of soldiers and Indians were close behind. Webb panicked. He ordered British forts guarding the Great Carrying Place to be set afire, gathered his people, and scurried back to Albany.

The story of the tattered Union Jack and the butchery at Fort Oswego was unpleasant news for colonists and British. General Webb's fear-ridden retreat seemed to them as craven as Colonel Dunbar's flight to Philadelphia after Braddock's defeat. The Earl of Loudoun, looking for a scapegoat, blamed Shirley. Shirley was deeply implicated, but placing the entire blame on him was like charging a member of Noah's family with causing the Great Flood because he predicted rain.

Blunders and defeats in America and in Europe were costing Britain prestige. But in December, 1756, one of England's greatest and most famous statesmen came to power as Secretary of State. This was William Pitt, later first Earl of Chatham, who despite ups and downs was certain he knew how to win the war.

CHAPTER 14

1757, DISMAL YEAR FOR BRITAIN

PITT's early life was difficult. As a student at Eton and Oxford, he was plagued by bad health, and it dogged him after he left school. Nevertheless, he sought both a military and political career.

In the House of Commons at twenty-seven, Pitt quarreled with every colleague showing promise. They found him vain and disagreeable but extremely talented, a fearless, quick-thinking adversary who could whip acid into his speeches. Most English leaders of the period were noted for their haughtiness, and few exceeded William Pitt. By the time this energetic man rose to power as Secretary of State, even King George II hated him.

The paradox of Pitt was that he reached thousands of people and inspired them, "down to the powder-monkeys on the battleships, to the little shopkeepers, to the youngest officer of the line." So wrote Sir Winston Churchill of William Pitt, almost two centuries later. Pitt may have been Churchill's model. Both united public opinion behind them in times of crisis. England needed strong direction in late 1756. She was losing on every front.

When Pitt stepped into power, he said he was going to "rouse England from a condition so feeble that twenty thousand men from France could shake her." But to accomplish this he had to manipulate British politics.

To ready Britain, he re-equipped and reorganized the navy, but then he rode off in many directions, squandering men and money. This was sad because Pitt had drive, ability, and large ideas of empire.

He now threw a log in Loudoun's wagon wheels by ordering him to capture the powerful fortress at Louisbourg.

Loudoun wondered what would happen next. He was already committed to Oswego, and he had to hold the Hudson Valley–Lake George route. Part of Pitt's difficulty was that, although he had a quick, nimble brain, he was an amateur general.

The Earl of Loudoun carried out his orders. Six thousand regulars answered to him when, in May, 1757, he sailed from New York for Halifax on his perilous mission. It was dangerous not only because of the enemy, but because he was barging into a latitude where summer lingers only a few days. He was delayed at Halifax while waiting for more men and ships. This was in a day when ships traveled at unpredictable speeds because of variations in wind power. Loudoun was not idle. While he waited, he tried to improve his soldiers by giving realistic training in siege operations.

The earl assembled a council of war. It droned on and on for nine wearisome days, accomplishing nothing but pages of minutes—that made torpid reading when Pitt eventually pored over them in London.

Finally, in August, 1757, with fogs shrouding the coast, British ships captured a French schooner. After questioning the enemy sailors, the British admiral, Francis Holburne, estimated the fortress as being too powerful to attack. Loudoun accepted this and called off the expedition, sailing for New York. This required moral courage on his part because recently Admiral John Byng had faced a firing squad in London for "failing to do his Utmost."

Benjamin Franklin said the campaign against Louisbourg was "frivolous, expensive . . . a disgrace to our Nation beyond Conception."

While the Earl of Loudoun hesitated before Louisbourg, the dashing French general Montcalm led ten thousand men (two thousand of them Indians) toward the most northern British stronghold, Fort William Henry, New York. Loudoun believed, before sailing for Halifax, that he had left the northern frontier secure, but he failed to realize the extent of Montcalm's energy. The dynamic Frenchman was out to translate work, sacrifice, and personal self-denial into victory. In his dash into New York, he wanted no trailside picnics, no lavish arrangements for himself. He ordered his soldiers to travel light, and he set the example: a bearskin for a mattress or cover was good enough for him.

When Montcalm neared Fort William Henry, he sent a column to cut communications between it and Fort Edward, seven miles away, where the inert General Webb had four thousand men.

Montcalm's artillery pounded Fort William Henry for six days, and no hint of rescue came from General Webb. On the contrary, he was lowering morale at Fort Edward by sending his personal belongings back to Albany. Finally, when the white flag went up at William Henry, scenes developed that were worse than the horrors of Oswego. When the fort surrendered, Montcalm's officers quickly told the British to pour all rum on the ground. Some disobeyed, and the Indians drank all they could hold.

Shortly, the drunken Indians attacked, and eighty-seven sick and wounded were sliced like meat in a butcher's shop. Montcalm and some of his officers risked their lives by running into the center of the butchery, yelling to make the Indians stop. Montcalm bared his breast and shouted, "You break your promises! Kill me first!"

The slaughter stopped for a while. Then sixteen hundred prisoners, with women and children, marched with a French escort, under a red flag, for Fort Edward. (Because the French flag was white, the French used red for a flag of truce.) The prisoners felt they were fortunate; Montcalm had extracted a pledge from them that they would not bear arms against France for eighteen months, and they were being exchanged for Frenchmen and Indians held by the British.

Suddenly Indians, led by Abnaki warriors, charged out of the forest, shouting the "death halloo." Down went prisoners, women and children, as tomahawks and scalping knives worked. Some of the French guards protested and received wounds from the Indians. The savages ripped the clothes from the prisoners they left alive. When Montcalm and his officers heard of this, they feared loss of prestige for France when the news reached the Continent.

Montcalm now returned to Montreal and Quebec. He had decided not to push farther south from Fort William Henry because he knew he would be outnumbered. Also, his Indians and Canadian militia had taken their booty and had gone home.

In reality Montcalm's attack on Fort William Henry was only a raid. However, British spirits sank. General Webb's fright and his lack of daring, as well as the fiasco Loudoun staged before Louisbourg, made the British wonder if the French were eventually going to control America.

Bad news continued. A September hurricane, called "the most furious ever known in the history of man," wrecked almost all of the British fleet blockading Louisbourg. (Down, too, went three powerful French ships.)

Then, just before winter howled in, French and Indians raided a Palatine settlement at German Flats (near present-day Herkimer, New York). About 50 German scalps were lifted, and 150 people trekked into captivity after their livestock had been slaughtered, their barns and houses burned. These were people who had wanted to be neutral.

But in spite of the dismal news, the subjects of King George II found time to chuckle. In late December, 1757, Robert Rogers was ordered to scout Ticonderoga and to capture a prisoner. The ranger brought back two. Before he returned, he tried to lure the French out of their fort into an ambush. When he failed, he killed seventeen cattle tethered nearby, and set fire to lumber and a pile of charcoal. He tied a note addressed to the fort's commandant on the horns of a cow:

. . . I thank you for the fresh meat you have sent me; I shall take care of my prisoners. I request you present my compliments to the Marquis de Montcalm.

Rogers
Commandant of Independent Companies

The French commandant called this "ill-timed braggadocio."

Near the end of the dismal year for the British, William Pitt recalled the Earl of Loudoun. But events more terrible would occur that would have to be absorbed by the British and their colonists. Pitt precipitated them when he gave Loudoun's command to General James Abercromby. Pitt selected him because he had influential friends. It was a disastrous way to select a general.

CHAPTER 15

A WOODEN GENERAL
AGAINST A WOODEN WALL

JAMES ABERCROMBY was a terrible general to inflict on an army. He was a stolid, set-in-his-way product of thirty-one years in the British Army. Frosty as an October morning in the mountains, he was unapproachable and suspicious. He found it impossible to adjust to American warfare. He was fifty and acted older. Perhaps he had little self-confidence in spite of his long service. In addition, ill health bogged him down.

Abercromby did have a most capable second-in-command in young Lord Howe. George Howe had gained the imagination of the Army by traveling into enemy country with Major Robert Rogers to see how the rangers operated. Howe returned filled with enthusiasm for the rangers. He was smart, alert, and saw the worth of Americans. Lord Howe seemed to live in a different world from the senior general.

When Pitt bowed to politics by appointing Abercromby to high command, he hoped Howe would be an anchor to windward for the dull Scot, and that Abercromby would use Howe's brains. Unfortunately for the Redcoats and colonials, things did not work that way.

"Mrs. Nabby Cromby," as his men nicknamed him, was to fight General Montcalm, impetuous leader—excitable and nervous at times, but cool in a crisis.

General Louis de Montcalm worried in July, 1758, as he paced Fort Carillon. The fort, called Ticonderoga by the British, guarded the portage between Lake Champlain and Lake George. Montcalm felt uneasy. His Indians had returned from scouting to the southern end of Lake George saying the enemy there was as thick as red leaves in the fall and that Abercromby's army was obviously headed for Fort Carillon.

A story goes that a month before, there had been a clash between partisans. Major Rogers and three men had been making a map (probably notes on the terrain) along the Ticonderoga River, at Howe's request. Not far away, a British captain led thirty-five men, also on reconnaissance. Suddenly, shots and war whoops shattered the quiet of the forest like a storm. Rogers saw "between thirty and fifty" French and Indians attacking the British party. The enemy was led by the daring Canadian light infantryman, Lieutenant Wolff.

Rogers and his three men tore through the woods to help the hard-pressed Redcoats. In the skirmish, when the British were retreating to their boats, Rogers received a minor flesh wound in the leg but escaped. Because of this,

Canadian Indians said he lived a charmed life, and called him "White Devil."

When Montcalm paced the ramparts of Fort Carillon, wondering what to do, he resembled a figure in a colorful print. A black felt tricornered hat, edged with gold lace and short white feathers, crowned his head. A long blue coat, sporting oversized cuffs and gleaming with gold lace, covered most of his red waistcoat and breeches. Jackboots made him look taller. Montcalm was an eagle in bright plumage.

The French leader made a wise decision. He would not wait in the fort for a British attack. It was not, he thought, the place for a last-ditch stand. True, his king had spent a fortune on the place, with graft oozing into the pockets of crooks, but Montcalm believed it too small for his 3,600 soldiers. Consequently, he ordered them to build a loopholed log wall, varying in height from waist to eight feet high, zigzagging across a ridge about a mile and a half back from Lake Champlain. When the wall was finished, he strengthened it with sandbags. Trees were felled and placed with branches pointing toward the enemy to block the approaches.

On July 5, 1758, the enemy came. Abercromby had about 6,300 Redcoats and 9,500 volunteers from New York, Connecticut, Rhode Island, and New Jersey. They rode up Lake George on a magnificent flotilla of nine hundred bateaux and 135 whaleboats, with rafts carrying artillery—the water movement under command of newly promoted Lieutenant Colonel Bradstreet. It was the finest army every seen on the American continent.

At noon the next day, in a preliminary fight between outguards, Lord Howe, brave and beloved, collapsed with a bullet through his breast. Howe had been called "the brains of the army." Certainly, Abercromby could ill afford such a loss.

July 8 was a perfect northern New York summer's day, with Lake Champlain looking like an oil painting. Not a cloud graced the sky. General Abercromby ordered his men to smash headlong against the wall. They marched, the shrieking, skirling music of the bagpipes in the Black Watch Regiment spurring men forward. The pipers carried broadswords and expected to use them. Pounding drums set the tempo. The massive array seemed almost to guarantee victory.

Montcalm's soldiers manned the loopholes. The uniforms of his men were even gaudier than those of the soldiers marching toward them in the deathly parade. Suddenly, French muskets cracked, tearing the attackers apart. Down went squads of Britons and Americans. The noise sounded through the beautiful hills as if heaven itself were enraged. Survivors reeled back, carrying what wounded they could.

Abercromby seemed to lose his head. In a short time, he ordered another attack against the wall. Again it came, the bagpipes crying in a high-pitched whine. Abercromby was not using his artillery against the wooden barrier. His engineer officer had never seen anything like Montcalm's wall, and his solution, offered to Abercromby and accepted, was *Charge!*

Abercromby desperately missed the advice of young Lord Howe. Thomas Gage was second-in-command, but his mind froze as soon as the fight started.

In five assaults, soldiers of the English king carried out the stupid, suicidal orders of Abercromby to smash straight ahead against the wall. For King George II, the attacks proved a grievous loss. When the fighting was over, sixteen hundred men were killed, wounded, or missing.

The terrible fault came to roost at Abercromby's tent. He had artillery and troops enough to attack from other directions, or cut around behind, with Bradstreet and Rogers to lead these maneuvers, but Abercromby used neither.

Thomas Mante, a soldier-author who fought in the war, wrote later:

> Britain never had an army whose claim to favor and protection was so just as that which served in America; and although Britain had been mortified with repeated accounts of disgraceful checks, her general officers, and not her soldiers, were the cause of them.

Mante clearly had Abercromby, as well as others, in mind.

After the battle, General Abercromby's broken army withdrew. Montcalm, now more revered than ever by his men, did not strike into the colonies. He was handicapped by lack of support from both the Canadian and the French governments and knew he would be disastrously outnumbered.

Before Montcalm left for Canada, he ordered a towering wooden cross placed near the center of the wall. Today it exists in stone. Another most unusual memorial, its cost paid by the Massachusetts Bay Colony, was erected in Westminster Abbey in honor of young Lord Howe, reading, "In testimony of the sense they had of his services and military virtues, and of the affection their officers and soldiers bore his command."

"Montcalm Congratulating His Victorious Troops after the Battle of Carillon, 1758." From a painting by H. A. Ogden.

Courtesy of the Fort Ticonderoga Museum

Abercromby was so badly shaken by the defeat that he sponsored a daring scheme, already approved in London. John Bradstreet had long nursed it. Consequently, Abercromby gave him 2,652 soldiers and 300 bateaumen for a very dangerous venture: a thrust north along Lake Ontario to capture Fort Frontenac.

The odd part of the plan was that Bradstreet would pay all expenses of the expedition, and if successful he would be reimbursed and recommended for promotion!

Bradstreet's men believed in him because of his brains and forceful personality. He was even known to the enemy as "a famous expediter of transportation."

Colonel Bradstreet ordered all hands to keep quiet about the plan, but when he started, Iroquois Indians dashed ahead to warn the French at Fort Frontenac. Before word of the outcome of the risky venture reached Pitt in London, the King's minister received startling news of Louisbourg.

CHAPTER 16

BRITAIN'S FLAG RISES

"WRYNECKED DICK" BOSCAWEN paced his quarterdeck off Louisbourg. A fresh spring breeze whipped whitecaps on the green breakers to a froth. His flagship and 156 other warships and transports tugged at their anchors in Gabarus Bay. Louisbourg lay a mile and a half to starboard. Herring gulls shrieked as they rode air currents above the flagship as if to warn, "Rocks ahead."

At various times in the last three years Admiral Edward Boscawen had commanded warships that partially blocked French shipping slipping in and out of the St. Lawrence and the fortress. Blockade duty was hard duty. The sailors hated it—too far from home. In addition, the weather was as rough as the water, and when you had your warships spread in a vast net to catch the French, storms and squalls

howled out of the north and scattered your ships as if they
were chips in a millrace.

In a cabin on the *Namur*, 90 guns, sat General Jeffery
Amherst, a methodical but bulldog type of leader who
nine months before had starred as rear-guard commander
at the Battle of Hastenbeck in Europe. Pitt believed Amherst possessed ability and rescued him from a staff desk.
Then Pitt told him tersely, almost abruptly, to team with
Admiral Boscawen to seize Louisbourg, one of the strongest defense works in the world. Twenty-five years and
millions of francs had gone into its construction. To capture it, Amherst and Boscawen had 12,260 soldiers, sailors,
and marines.

With Amherst on the *Namur*, poring over sketchy
charts of the coast and sipping a mixture of ginger, sugar,
and water, sat Brigadier James Wolfe, one of the best
combat leaders in the British Army. (See Appendix II for
explanation of the term "brigadier.") Both officers had
reconnoitered the craggy shore in small boats to search
for landing places. Compared to the older and stronger-
built Amherst, the quiet Wolfe looked like a sickly student. He was paler than usual, a poor sailor.

The physical appearance of the two men did not reflect
their true characteristics. Amherst was not a dashing front-
line type. On the contrary, he wanted every move carefully coordinated, down to the moment of fixing bayonets. He was a silent man, courteous to subordinates,
ordinarily cautious, but capable on rare occasions of great
daring. He had organized the expedition in Halifax.
There, some of his Redcoats had strayed around the
countryside and had been murdered by savages. This had
been Amherst's first brush with Indians, and it had made

a deep impression, one that would tell later. He had little use for Indians.

Brigadier Wolfe stood at the other end of the leadership spectrum from Jeffery Amherst. James Wolfe was capable of inspiring people within sight and sound, although ill health had always dogged him. He was dynamic in spite of his frail looks. He had been in the Army since he was fourteen and witnessed his first battle at sixteen. His reputation for boldness was firmly established. It was this characteristic that caused King George II to say, when someone ventured that Wolfe was mad, "Mad? I hope he bites some of my other generals."

The roll of the flagship made the lantern, suspended from an oak beam above the table in the cabin, perform an erratic dance. Landing on the hostile shore seemed as uncertain as the swing of the lamp. Amherst, though, had a factor in his favor: young Brigadier Wolfe was going ashore with the first wave.

For six days the fleet wallowed in the offshore swell. Fogs in the morning cleared in the afternoon. A squall threw the warship *Trent* against the rocks. The days were tense for the men who would storm ashore, and just as taut for the men who would meet them.

On June 8, 1758, the weather changed. The target was plainly visible in the sunrise: the fortress protected by the French fleur-de-lis banner and rows of guns. The moment had arrived. Warships thundered against fire on the beach defenses. Shortly, a flotilla of whaleboats and flat-bottomed craft streamed for beaches inside the harbor, four miles from Louisbourg's stone ramparts.

James Wolfe stood before the mast of a catboat skimming along in the center of the onrushing small craft, his

"Major General James Wolfe, Commander in Chief of His Majesty's Forces on the Expedition Against Quebec." Mezzotint by R. Houston after J. S. C. Schaak. *Courtesy B. T. Batsford Ltd. and National Portrait Gallery, London*

red hair plaited into a queue and sticking out behind like a narrow rudder. His inherent braggadocio was evident in his personal armament. He carried a cane.

When the landing craft pulled into range, French batteries opened. Yet the tars tugged hard at the oars. At closer range, muskets barked, pouring bullets into the soldiers and the backs of the sailors.

Wolfe judged the casualties as heavy. He was on the verge of signaling "Return!" when three boats bearing Lieutenants Thomas Brown and Thomas Hopkins and Ensign Allan Grant disappeared in a cove. In a few minutes, the lieutenants and their soldiers had clambered to the top of a little headland and fired at the French. Wolfe signaled with his cane. His craft and a half dozen small boats veered toward the cove. Redcoat soldiers and General Wolfe jumped into the surf and scrambled ashore to fight. This was the beginning of the end of Louisbourg.

Amherst ordered British artillery floated ashore, and shortly cannonades thundered at shorter range at the 219 cannon and 17 mortars in Louisbourg. The French, outnumbered, fought hard. It was 4,000 French and Canadians plus "2,600 seamen and Indians" against the 11,000 or 12,000 attackers. In addition, parts of Louisbourg's walls were crumbling. The French had neglected to fortify strongly the nearby ridges. Worse, the morale of the defenders was low and the French Navy not powerful enough.

A few nights after the landing, British sailors staged a daring night raid near the fortress to sink the French warship *Prudent*. Then a cannonball from one of the British ships struck the powder magazine on a French warship. It exploded. Other French men-of-war caught fire, and the French fleet anchored in the harbor was reduced from twelve to two ships.

During the siege of the fortress, there was a brief return to the customs of chivalry. Governor Augustine de Drucourt, senior in Louisbourg, was permitted to send letters and clothing, under a red flag, to Frenchmen who had been captured. When Amherst sent the governor's wife pineapples, recently in from the West Indies, the French couple sent back fifty bottles of champagne and tubs of butter. But soldiers on both sides, facing death, knew nothing of the exchange of gracious niceties.

On the forty-eighth day of the siege, July 26, 1758, a red flag went up in the center of the fortress and the French surrendered. This capture was a tremendous victory for the British, of enormous psychological importance. It was the turning point of the war. No longer would Louisbourg stand guard near the entrance of the

St. Lawrence; no longer would it be a base for French codfishers and a harbor for French privateers, supply ships, and warships.

When news of the fall of the fortress arrived in London, salutes were fired, bonfires were lighted, and captured flags were carried through the streets to St. Paul's. Two years later, Pitt sent word to America for Louisbourg to be leveled.

While Wolfe was leading attacks against Louisbourg, the remarkable Lieutenant Colonel Bradstreet headed the expedition Abercromby had approved to the northernmost reaches of Lake Ontario against Fort Frontenac.

The dynamic, British-born colonel led his soldiers and bateaumen up the Mohawk, past the Great Carrying Place, where his comrades were rebuilding a fort. Bradstreet pressed on past the black ruins of Oswego. When he embarked with his men on the lake, they were fortunate indeed that the French naval force controlling Ontario was not on the alert.

Although the Iroquois had warned Fort Frontenac that Colonel Bradstreet was coming, he captured the fort after it put up a surprisingly light defense. Governor Pierre François de Vaudreuil of Canada, son of the Vaudreuil who had ordered the raid on Deerfield, sent an expedition to help, but it arrived too late. Frontenac turned out to be a shell of a fort, a huge but lightly held storehouse.

For the Crown, Bradstreet seized seventy-six cannon, seven unrigged ships, and bales of furs worth £30,000. He not only destroyed the fort, but also about £800,000 worth of supplies he could not carry back to Albany. The loss of the supplies hurt the French. It cost them food, presents for Indians in the Ohio Valley, and trading goods for their forts there.

The capture of Fort Frontenac impressed the Indians, especially the Iroquois. In addition, Bradstreet kept two of the best vessels of the French fleet and put them in condition to give the British control over Lake Ontario. Although John Bradstreet could not know it, his capture of the tremendous warehouse that was Fort Frontenac aided a thrust Pitt had ordered to the south against the fort whose soldiers had defeated Braddock. This involved the unusual leader "Ironhead" Forbes.

CHAPTER 17

IRONHEAD FORBES

G EORGE WASHINGTON was in a predicament. Ironhead Forbes tired him out and irritated him.

Washington, a regimental commander in 1758, was extremely anxious to play an important role in the strike against Fort Duquesne. Pitt had ordered it, and Washington knew its importance. But Washington found himself in disagreement about strategy with the leader of the expedition, Brigadier John "Ironhead" Forbes, at the time when Amherst and Boscawen's men were battling for Louisbourg.

Forbes possessed an iron will. He was a cheery Scot and, fortunately for Washington, a fair-minded leader who was not upset when a subordinate had different views. He had positive ideas. He disapproved of the method poor Braddock had used against the fort at the Forks of the Ohio:

laboriously carving a road through the forest. But Forbes's idea involved even slower progress. He planned to build a series of forts through the forest toward Duquesne, in reality a chain of supply bases, each helping the one farther west.

Washington objected. "Far too slow," he said to Colonel Henry Bouquet, a Swiss officer serving in the British Army, second-in-command of the expedition, and Forbes's close friend. When Washington's thoughts were swept aside like dust, he assumed a gloomy outlook and called Forbes's ideas backward. Washington believed the plan far too tedious for their Indian allies. "They will desert," he predicted.

Washington was right. Most of the 400 Cherokees, up from South Carolina under their famous chief Attakulla-culla, were attracted by thoughts of fighting French and their Indians, as well as by £6,000 worth of presents they heard would be given out. The Cherokees were not for building roads or forts. They wanted action. There is reason to believe they also hesitated to push toward Duquesne because they found they would come into conflict with the Shawnees. The two tribes were then at peace.

Before the Cherokees pulled out for South Carolina, their leader told Brigadier Forbes, "You will find no one at Fort Duquesne." Word of this had been filtering in, but Forbes could not depend on rumors. He pushed ahead in his careful, methodical way, angry at the Cherokee deserters.

The next thing irritating John Forbes was a letter Washington wrote a friend. Its critical tone was unkind to Forbes:

. . . All is lost by Heavens! Our enterprize is ruined. . . . We will find the Southern Indians against us, and these colonies desolated.

Forbes found the letter. (It may have been left so he would see it.) Fortunately for Washington's career, the evenhanded Scotsman did not become angry. But after Forbes read the letter he placed little confidence in Washington. This did not change Washington's opinion; he could be as stubborn as the Scot.

Even though George Washington questioned Brigadier Forbes's plan, others did not, and many admired him. Forbes was as remarkable as Washington. He labored patiently with the politicians of Pennsylvania, Virginia, Maryland, and North Carolina to secure troops, supplies, money, and transportation; he was polite and understanding, and he gradually secured most of what he needed. In addition, Forbes was about a century ahead of the average military leader of the time because he believed that a leader must be considerate of his men. He also wanted his soldiers to be able to fight like Indians and American rangers, as well as in powerful mass formation.

After much hassling, Forbes started west from Carlisle, Pennsylvania. Neither he nor Bouquet cared where supplies came from as long as they got them. Forbes was ill, suffering from what was probably dysentery, yet he worked as hard as anyone on the march.

Jealousy hampered the expedition. Pennsylvania, Maryland, and Virginia all claimed the Ohio Valley. Virginians wanted Forbes to use Braddock's old road, so it would be available for their use after the war. They did not want Pennsylvanians to have a new road into the valuable western territories.

When Forbes crawled west, after solving the trying problem of obtaining wagons, he benefited from the work of the unusual trader and Indian agent, George Croghan. Two years before, William Johnson had ordered Croghan to Pennsylvania to keep Indians friendly, to settle grievances of the Delawares and Shawnees over the failure of Pennsylvania to build a fort on the Ohio, and to weaken the loyalty of the Ohio tribes to the King of France. Croghan's monument is that he performed his main mission with little money and in the face of Pennsylvania politics. His work now helped Forbes.

Another advance agent whose work assisted Forbes even more was a missionary from a Moravian sect, Christian Frederick Post. Pennsylvania politicians had requested that Post go into the forest to ask Indians to respect the old treaties with England. Post refused until he was persuaded that it would be in the interest of peace. When he appeared before the wooden walls of Fort Duquesne, the French wanted to take him prisoner, but the Indians protested. They were beginning to believe in Post and his preaching.

The Indian agent and the missionary helped, but it was Forbes's will that brought his army west through all hazards. By this time Forbes was so ill he had to be carried on a litter suspended between two horses. The Indians called him "Ironhead," and if they were referring to his strength of character, it was an apt nickname.

A terrible incident occurred en route to the fort. Colonel Bouquet sent Major James Grant and 840 soldiers ahead—

not to fight but to take prisoners and gain information. Bouquet was beating off the Indians harassing his part of the expedition, and he thought Grant capable of getting information that would prevent this and help capture the fort.

Near Duquesne, Grant's men were discovered. Out of the fort poured French and Indians, and Grant lost one third of his men. The fight stunned Forbes's column—as much as Braddock's defeat had rocked English-speaking people. Still Forbes pressed on, although Grant's loss caused more Indians to desert.

Forbes marched on, arriving at Fort Duquesne on November 24, 1758—only to find it a charred mess. The French had blown it up the day before because they realized they would be outnumbered and because they lacked supplies. The scarcity of food and other items there was a direct result of John Bradstreet's capture of the warehouses at Fort Frontenac.

When Forbes's army examined the wrecked Duquesne, they felt sick. A row of stakes in the ashes were crowned with the heads of Grant's men who had been captured.

In addition, Brigadier Forbes was mortally ill. Before he was carried to Philadelphia, where he died, he left Lieutenant Colonel Hugh Mercer, a Pennsylvania physician, in command at the Forks of the Ohio. Mercer examined sites for a new fort. The gallant Forbes wrote Pitt:

I have used the freedom of giving your name to Ft. DuQuesne. . . . Your spirits now make us masters of the Place.

And so Pittsburgh took her place on American maps.

In the summer of 1759, the British attacked Fort Niagara, near the western end of Lake Ontario. The French commander, Captain François Pouchot, was a journalist. He wrote:

> . . . some of [our] Indian scouts [fell] upon a guard of English who were watching 22 bateaux they had carried over by land. The Indians killed a dozen, and having cut off their heads, set them on poles. This event led to others.

Pouchot's Fort Niagara looked strong, but it wasn't. The British invested it in continental style, digging zigzag approach trenches that inched closer and closer. The second-in-command of the attackers, Sir William Johnson, led about 1,000 Iroquois he had gathered after much oratory on the banks of the Mohawk. The Iroquois now said they were anxious to fight for Johnson and the King of England. They believed the British were winning, and if they did, there would be a good chance for furs to flow again from the west. Then they could again collect tolls.

In the besieged fort, Captain Pouchot felt relieved when a scout slipped in and told him a rescue column was coming from Montreal. But the British ambushed it, and the Indians chased the Frenchmen in the relief force about five miles, in a grisly run, hacking at them with tomahawks and scalping knives.

Before Fort Niagara fell, William Johnson became the leader of the attack, as Britain's Brigadier John Prideaux died in an accident. It is to Johnson's credit that he controlled his Iroquois when the red flag went up.

A minor drama was unfolding at the same time in Quebec. The French capital was in severe distress, troubled with a runaway inflation, and a citizenry existing on a starvation diet. Part of the difficulty was that Vaudreuil had failed to stop crooked politicians who put defense funds in their own pockets.

In addition, in this summer of 1759, Quebec citizens recognized the threat of superior British military power. On the St. Lawrence, about five miles below the town, a tremendous fleet of 49 warships and 119 transports dropped anchor. General James Wolfe, hero of the Louisbourg landing, was in command of the expedition. The naval leader was Vice Admiral Charles Saunders. They teamed well, but on September 2 the situation so frustrated Wolfe that he wrote Pitt he did not know what to do. It seemed almost impossible to capture Quebec.

CHAPTER 18

BLUEJACKETS AND REDCOATS
AT QUEBEC

IN June, 1759, citizens of Quebec gathered on the cliff of the upper town to gaze at the tremendous British fleet. Many French and Canadians were amazed.

Difficulties of navigating the St. Lawrence had long been considered part of the city's defenses, but for several days enemy warships had dropped anchor below the city, out of range of its guns. Redcoats were rowing to an island to set up camp. The Union Jack floated over 49 men-of-war and about 119 other sailing vessels serving as troopships.

The pennant of Admiral Saunders fluttered from the mast of one of the powerful three-decker, 90-gun ships, the *Neptune*.

Most citizens of the city, but not all, had faith in the dashing, impetuous, warmhearted Montcalm. No one was more loyal to the King of France than the hero of Fort Carillon (Ticonderoga). But Montcalm's difficulties with Governor de Vaudreuil were common knowledge around town and in the soldiers' camps, and not all of the blame for the friction could be assigned to the governor. Montcalm had worked to undermine him.

For at least two years, Montcalm had realized Quebec would come under attack. When word arrived from France that an enemy fleet was sailing for Canada, he hurried work on the defenses. He assembled fireships, about 14,000 soldiers, and "some Indians." Montcalm strengthened defenses everywhere around the city except across the river and to the west. Like his opponent, Wolfe, he was more effective in front-line combat than in an office.

A few nights after the fleet anchored, Montcalm ordered the fireships cut loose. Downriver they floated, decks and holds crammed with combustible material, powder, and grenades. Fortunately for the British, fuses had not been lighted smartly, and the attack fizzled.

General Wolfe countered by ordering a bombardment of the town. Shot and shell arched into Quebec, wrecking homes and shops. The cathedral caught fire. This bombardment was to last sixty-eight days, but the pounding the city absorbed failed to help the attackers. Wolfe had hoped it would draw Montcalm's men away from the town so a battle could be fought.

A month later, at night, more volcanoes floated toward the British fleet. Like the first foray, the fireships were loaded at great cost to France. Blazes, shooting upward into the darkness, and sounds of the explosions were terrifying. However, brave tars rowed out to the fireships, grappled them with iron hooks, and towed them harmlessly ashore. The sailors said later, "We took Hell in tow."

The Redcoats looked to Wolfe to counter French moves and to win. At Pitt's order, Wolfe was now a major general, but as the leader of the expedition, he was not as confident or as dashing as when he went ashore with the first wave at Louisbourg. His obligations weighed on him. He had never had so much responsibility, and in giving it to him Pitt was gambling.

The strategy of how to take Quebec rested with Wolfe, and the resultant pressure rattled him. Part of the trouble was that he was ill. Numerous bottles of medicine lay stacked in his kit, but neither they nor his doctors cured his ailments. Nothing seemed certain to the irritable string-bean of a general, except that taking the city was a Herculean task. Nevertheless, he drove himself. Like Forbes, he was doing his duty with death's hand on his shoulder. Wolfe not only yearned to carry out his mission, but he was determined to make his mark in history.

James Wolfe was still the "soldiers' friend," as some of his Redcoats called him. He had ordered that their uniforms be cut more comfortably, and he outlawed the cat-o'-nine-tails. He believed discipline could be maintained by humane methods.

Much of the pressure on Wolfe came from the way the summer was slipping away. Vice Admiral Saunders would have to withdraw the fleet before ice locked it in, and ice had appeared in the St. Lawrence in November.

Before General Wolfe wrote Pitt on September 2, 1759, that he did not know what to do, he had tried a number

"View of the Attack of the French Fire Ships on the British Fleet in Quebec, 1759." Oil by Dominic Serres, copied after Samuel Scott.
Courtesy the Public Archives of Canada

of things in addition to the ceaseless bombardment, and each had failed. The campaign became a grindstone honing his ambition to a fine edge.

He had launched an infantry attack across the inlet near the beautiful falls of Montmorency, northeast of Quebec, but someone erred in figuring the flow of the tide. Thus the soldiers' boats grounded on the mud flats—sitting ducks for Montcalm's artillery. Grenadiers and the Royal American Regiment splashed ashore and scrambled almost one by one to the top of the bluff. French guns cut down five hundred.

Wolfe had to shoulder the blame for the huge loss. He stood before the surviving grenadiers, lashing them with his tongue and tugging fretfully at his coat sleeve, as if he thought he could lengthen it. He believed the grenadiers had started the disorderly rush to the top of the cliff. The grenadiers resented being shot at and then tongue-lashed.

Morale started to slide downhill, but the men kept a hard face toward the French.

By September 2, General Wolfe had become difficult to live with. He blew up at Major George Scott and handed him the same treatment he had handed the grenadiers. At Wolfe's order, Scott had led a strong force of regulars, rangers, and seamen against Canadian guerrilla bands. Although Scott raided all along the river, Montcalm remained in Quebec's entrenchments.

Wolfe, nervous and ill, hurt the rangers by dressing them down for a poor performance. Then he struck out at Major Scott, and Scott talked back. This shook up Wolfe. Scott's contemporaries said he could do this and escape a penalty because he was the son of a friend of Wolfe's mother.

Wolfe's next exhibition of temper was caused by one of his three excellent brigadiers, George Townshend. Townshend, Wolfe's friend and as bold as Scott, thought the general a subject for cartoons. He drew a skillful pen-and-ink sketch showing a soldier of the Cromwell period sitting slumped beneath a grinning caricature of Wolfe. The drawing stressed Wolfe's receding chin. The caption read, "Shades of Cromwell. Has England come to this?" Next, the brigadier drew a picture accentuating Wolfe's skinny build, showing a staff officer measuring Wolfe's height. The cartoon bore the label, "Higher than before! Our general begins his day."

Wolfe, not too sure of himself and probably suffering from an inferiority complex, possibly because of his face, figure, and undistinguished family background, was stung by the laughter around the headquarters. He snapped at his friend Townshend, saying that after the war he might request the satisfaction of a duel.

All the while, parts of his army were dueling at close range with the enemy. Sentries were being knifed, scalped, and mutilated. Wolfe ripped out the order: "It is all right to scalp Indians and Canadians dressed like Indians."

In early August, Wolfe became even more frustrated when he sent Brigadier James Murray upstream with twelve hundred soldiers. The idea was to draw Montcalm's army out of the city. But Murray burned French supplies and operated forty miles above Quebec, too far for Montcalm to be lured away.

When Wolfe sent his dismal letter to Pitt saying he did not know what to do, the situation was deadlocked. In addition, Wolfe did not have his men in position to stage a hard, smashing attack. They were in camps stretching out for seven miles.

General Wolfe had three competent brigadiers, but he had become so irritable that communication with anyone was difficult. Now in September he turned to them in desperation and asked their advice. They suggested he use the fleet to bypass the city's guns at night, land upstream, and attack Quebec from the west. Wolfe, who had excellent common sense, saw this was a gamble—if he was defeated the campaign would be ruined at least for the year—but he accepted the plan because he believed he could make it work. He picked as a landing place a small cove on the river's north bank, where a path led upward to the open fields just west of Quebec.

Wolfe's attack up the steep trail, after twenty-four British volunteers had captured Canadians guarding the path, is one of the best-known stories of the war. When his army gained the heights above the river, he was on Montcalm's supply line, a most serious thing for the French, because Quebec was starving.

Myths have grown up around Wolfe's conduct the night before the attack. The stories go that, while in a boat on the river, General Wolfe recited lines of Gray's "Elegy" that ended: "The paths of glory lead but to the grave." Wolfe did enjoy poetry, but the odds are that no matter how discouraged he had become, a daring front-line type like Wolfe would not depress his comrades with gloomy verse. Perhaps the stories sprang from the fact that he carried in his wallet a somewhat similar verse he had penned. Nevertheless, witnesses vowed later that they were in boats close to James Wolfe's craft and heard poetry.

When the two armies faced each other on the Plains of Abraham, they were led by somewhat similar leaders. Both men relished being where the danger was far more than directing operations and working on administration in a headquarters. Montcalm was no better at strategy than Wolfe. Had the brave French leader possessed strategic sense he would have at least fortified the far shore of the St. Lawrence, to make Saunders' ships pay a heavy toll to sail upstream, and he would have secured the western approaches to the city.

The whole British campaign led up to September 13, when about thirty-two hundred Redcoats faced approximately five thousand French, most of them in white uniforms. Every man on the Plains of Abraham that day realized that his life, as well as the campaign, was at stake.

The French were handicapped: Montcalm had weakened his best regiments by diluting them with ill-trained bodies of militia. In addition, the French leader and his key officers had been surprised; they now were dancing to a tune called by Wolfe. The Redcoats were also better trained.

When the lines closed, once more Wolfe was the Wolfe of Louisbourg. In directing the fight, he was only 130 yards from the French when a bullet smashed through his wrist. This was not enough to make this determined leader turn back for first aid.

The battle on the grassy plain was an infantryman's fight. Both sides were deficient in artillery. But the British, with their splendid Brown Bess muskets and their discipline, had the whip hand. When they fired volleys, the French lines recoiled—in spite of the fact that just behind them, astride a black horse, rode the Marquis de Montcalm.

This fearless, attractive, and beloved leader met his death when a cannonball from a 6-pounder plowed into him. He lived but a few hours. With his last breath he framed a message to Wolfe asking for protection for French prisoners. But another bullet had torn into Wolfe's breast and killed him too.

Montcalm's army was defeated, and Quebec quickly surrendered. The British marched into the wrecked city past its defensive works while remnants of the French Army retreated up the St. Lawrence. Part of the Redcoat success can be traced to Pitt. He had the British Navy ready to support the campaign.

On the day of the battle, another drama was about to start 250 miles to the south which, when it became known, intrigued Americans almost as much as the capture of Quebec. General Amherst, on that day, handed Robert Rogers, the greatest of all rangers, orders sending him 150 miles into enemy territory on his most daring mission.

CHAPTER 19

ROGERS' MOST FAMOUS RAID

IT takes little imagination to visualize the systematic General Amherst writing in his journal. In his tent, by candlelight, he penned in his meager way:

> I ordered a detachment of 220 Chosen men under the command of Major Rogers to go & destroy the St. Francis Indian Settlements . . . not letting any one but Major Rogers know what about or where he was going.

Rogers, energetic and animated, was in great contrast to the handsome blue-blooded Amherst. A green jacket covered the ranger's deep chest. The coat's lighter-green cuffs and lapels added a bright note. On his massive head sat a light infantryman's little black cap, boasting a gay

"Major Roger Rogers."
From an old mezzotint by
Joh. Martin Will.

Photo courtesy of
John R. Cuneo

plume like a squirrel's tail. He had the face of a pugilist, complete with battered nose. He had an owllike look about him. But he could run like a cat.

When Amherst wrote his paragraph giving Rogers his most challenging mission, he felt frustrated. The French had tricked him at Carillon and Crown Point by blowing up their forts and withdrawing just before he ordered his attack. But as angry as Amherst was, he did not push on to Canada like a conqueror. He stopped, and in his plodding way repaired the forts.

Amherst was nettled because the St. Francis Indians (Abnakis) had penetrated what he thought a clever subterfuge. He had ordered three officers to travel to the St. Lawrence to see how Wolfe's attack against Quebec was progressing. The three scouts were to deceive Indians they might encounter by pretending they were out to make peace. Amherst believed this would be a passport through

hostile territory. But the Indians saw through the scheme
and hurried two of the officers to St. Francis to give them
personal experience in torture. When word trickled back
to Amherst, he stormed around, claiming the Indians had
violated a flag of truce.

When Rogers received Amherst's unusual orders, he
assembled his rangers. He did not tell them they were to
traverse 150 miles of trackless country that had never been
mapped. Instead he said, "Overhaul your equipment good.
I'm taking you to Suagothel."

"Where's that?" a sergeant asked.

Rogers' blue eyes twinkled. "It's a far piece," he said,
laughing. "Tell you later." Rogers wanted secrecy, with
no chance for a deserter in Amherst's army to steal away
to alert the French that rangers were on the way north on
Lake Champlain.

Many British officers looked down on colonial soldiers,
and some despised the rangers. Once, before his death,
General James Wolfe had announced, with a nervous tug
at his sleeve, "The Americans are the most con-
temptible cowardly dogs you can conceive." Wolfe had
called those who fought under Major George Scott "the
worst soldiers in the universe." But Rogers' Rangers were
well disciplined and carefully trained. They did what
Rogers told them to do; there was no time for debate in
the quick flash of an ambush. Later, Wolfe learned to put
considerable trust in the rangers.

Rogers took care of his men. For example, it was difficult for a paymaster to pay rangers because they were
often away from camp. Sometimes Rogers paid them from
his own pocket, a custom that would cause trouble when
he tried to collect from the Crown for men he had already

paid who were dead by the time the paymaster could settle their accounts. Rogers kept his vouchers and receipts in his head, and that was a mistake.

Rogers earned the admiration of his men by hard work. In addition, no mission was too dangerous for him. Success embellished the reputation of his rangers; their achievements gave Rogers the pick of incoming recruits.

On the way to St. Francis, before daybreak, Rogers ordered his men to pull their seventeen whaleboats into the woods and cover them with brush. Rogers could take no chance on being discovered by French patrol boats. With his men about him, Rogers squinted at a piece of paper he held in his powerful hands. "I'll read our orders from the general," he said, as calmly as if he were posting his men on camp guard.

. . . You will proceed to Missiquoi Bay (at the northern end of the lake) march & attack the enemy's settlement on the south side of the river St. Lawrence.

Remember the barbarities that have been committed by the enemy's Indian scoundrels [which they effected] without mercy. Take your revenge, but don't forget that tho' those villains have . . . murdered women & children of all ages, it is my orders that no women or children are killed or hurt.

[Afterward] join me wherever the army may be.

Your's, etc.

Jeff. Amherst

Sept. 13, 1759

The only noise was the caw of a crow. Rogers did not have to explain the orders. Each man had a personal interest in victory. The hard-looking group in trim green uniforms and blue Scotch bonnets, or tam-o'-shanters, knew the cruelties St. Francis Indians had inflicted for years on the New England frontier.

Rogers said, "If anyone wants to turn back instead of going on to Suagothel, I'll arrange it. That's my fancy name for St. Francis." His half-grin and his personality warmed each man like a campfire.

At night, the rangers rowed quietly up the lake, Rogers' whaleboat in the lead. When the weather turned cold and rainy, the rangers felt glad—this meant less chance of being discovered by a French patrol boat. Each morning when oncoming daylight streaked the sky in the east, Rogers led his column ashore. He was energetic. After the boats had been hidden in the forest for the day, he posted sentries, then waded into the water to look from the lake to see if any whaleboat was visible and to make sure tracks on the bank had been obliterated.

On the tenth day, before leaving Lake Champlain to hike overland, Rogers left two trusty Stockbridge Indians on guard over the branch-covered craft. "If the French find our boats," he told them, "you come to me fast. *On the run.*" Rogers was taking no chance of returning to an ambush.

The party, now down to 142 because of accidents and illnesses, struck north at a rapid rate. They avoided Indian trails, traveling through swamps and bogs so mucky they had difficulty keeping their moccasins on.

On the second day away from the lake, the two men the rangers least wanted to see appeared. The two Stockbridge Indians panted as they reported to Major Rogers, "French found boats! Four hundred men. On our trail."

Some leaders would have turned back to Amherst's army by a circuitous route, but not Rogers. His mission was to chastise the St. Francis Indians, and that was what he was going to do. Quickly, he planned a new route for the return trip: to the east, down the Connecticut River. He ordered Lieutenant Andrew McMullen to return to General Amherst at once with a message requesting that provisions be sent up the Connecticut to its junction with the Wells River (near present-day Woodsville, New Hampshire). "We'll need them bad on the return trip," Rogers said, impressing this on the lieutenant.

When McMullen reported to Amherst, the general gave the job of getting the provisions to the Wells River to Lieutenant Samuel Stevens.

Major Rogers now pressed on faster into enemy country. When the swift St. Francis River became a barrier, he succeeded in getting his men across by forming a human chain in the cold stream, using his biggest and strongest men to anchor it. On the twenty-second day of their trip, the tired rangers arrived at St. Francis village. Rogers hid his men. When night fell, he walked forward with two captains to plan the attack on the target.

They crept by lonely cabins on the outskirts and hid in brush. In the center of the little town stood poles decorated with about six hundred scalps. The three men saw the Indians enjoying a wild night of revelry, howling and dancing about fires to the beat of rattles and drums.

At three in the morning, Rogers woke the rangers. "Check your powder and put your packs aside," he said.

He posted forty men along a possible line of retreat the Indians might use. Then he loosed the whirlwind.

The rangers killed St. Francis Indians just as those Indians had slain New Englanders. The village was set on fire. After four hours of spreading hell, Rogers called off the raid and grouped his men for the rapid hike to the Connecticut River, over 170 miles away.

Rogers was aware that French and Indians would be after his rangers like angry hornets. On the eighth day of the rush for "home," he split his party into small groups to avoid enemy detachments trying to intercept him and to aid in hunting for food. Freezing November rains pelted the rangers and the enemy alike, but the rangers were at much greater disadvantage because their food supplies were almost exhausted.

The ghastly return trip of Rogers' rangers was highlighted by novelist, Kenneth Roberts, when he wrote of a ranger, whose party had been annihilated by French and Indians, telling Rogers, "They killed them all. They played ball with their heads."

Rogers' men were so hungry that killing a red squirrel was an event. Some rangers, without food for four days, ate their leather cartridge boxes and became sick. Rogers exuded no warmth now. He turned into a whip—a cat with nine tails—scourging his men on.

When Rogers' party reached the Wells River, the long-looked-forward-to rendezvous point, they found no food. There was nothing save the dying embers of a campfire. Rogers and his men could read the signs: the rescue party had given up hope and had departed. The spirit of the rangers slumped to its lowest point. Despair gripped them.

Not finding the food they needed seemed literally to be the end of the world.

Rogers made his men search for nuts and lily roots, scanty substitutes for nourishment. He ordered a raft built. This took time. Every hour added to their anxiety. While all concentrated on the raft, it was easy to visualize Canadian Indians sweeping out of the bushes with raised tomahawks.

When the raft was ready, Rogers, a captain, and an Indian boy climbed on it. "Keep hunting for food," Rogers told the men who were to wait while he and his two comrades went in search of help. "Hunt for roots, anything. Maybe you can kill a moose."

When the trio had floated to White River Falls on the rickety craft, they encountered a new problem. The raft charged over the crest and disintegrated. Rogers and his companions were fortunate to reach shore with their muskets.

The threesome worked to build yet another raft, but they were too weak to cut logs. Instead they burned them near proper lengths. This required a day. Fortunately, they sustained themselves by killing a partridge.

At another falls, the captain held the raft by a rope made of vines while Rogers swam in the icy pool below to catch their bundle of logs when it plunged over the top.

On the fifth day after leaving the Wells, Rogers discovered men cutting wood. Within half an hour a relief expedition was on the way upstream. Rogers hired men to search for stragglers, and two days later he rode upstream in a canoe laden with food for his people. This was the zenith of Robert Rogers' life.

Raiders do not win wars. Still, this raid was hailed all

over New England. No more would northern colonists have to live in fear of the St. Francis Indians. Most of the rangers returned, although some found graves in the forest.

General Amherst was very satisfied with Rogers and his raid, but an entry in his journal, written five days before Rogers reached the woodchoppers, evidenced the worry he had lived with:

> October 30, 1759. Very cold & frost. Lt. Stevens who I had sent with Provisions to meet Maj. Rogers Said there was no probability he would ever come back that way, but he should have waited longer.

Lieutenant Stevens faced a court-martial and was dismissed from the service.

Bad luck now began to follow Robert Rogers, and hounded him to the end of his days. He lost £800 belonging to the government when raiding Indians attacked Amherst's supply route. Other troubles with money, and with such people as Sir William Johnson and General Thomas Gage, hurt him.

Gage had long hated rangers because of their carefree ways—and probably their successes—and tried to undermine them, particularly Major Rogers, with General Amherst. When Rogers tried to purchase land along Lake George, he clashed with the interests of Sir William Johnson, now one of the most powerful and important men in America. Johnson claimed that area belonged to the Mohawks. Rogers believed this a cover-up—that Johnson wanted the land for himself. Johnson could stomach no rival, particularly one as famous as Rogers. Not long after the raid against St. Francis, Rogers gained two powerful enemies. In seven years, General Gage would be writing Sir William about Robert Rogers:

New York, Jan^{ry}. 13th. 1766

PRIVATE

. . . He is wild, vain, of little understanding, and of as little Principle; but withal has a share of Cunning, no Modesty or veracity and sticks at Nothing.

. . . He deserved Some Notice for his Bravery and readiness of Service . . . [however] he is some Thousands in Debt here. . . .

Gage was right: Robert Rogers was trapped by quicksands of debt.

But General Amherst saw Robert Rogers differently, and helped him all he could. In the fall of 1760, Amherst believed a show of British power would be helpful in calming western Indians, so he sent Rogers west at the head of two companies of rangers. The general also told Rogers, and others, that he wanted French arms collected and that Frenchmen were to be given the opportunity of taking the oath of allegiance to Britain. Presque Isle ("almost an island," or "peninsula") was Rogers' initial destination. It was a name French *voyageurs* applied to geographical places almost as often as American trappers applied "Rock Creek." This Presqu' Isle became the site of modern Erie, Pennsylvania.

On this trip, Rogers probably met an Indian leader whose star was definitely on the rise—the Ottawa chief Pontiac. But before Pontiac inspired western warriors, Amherst closed in on the French and Canadians.

CHAPTER 20

GENERAL AMHERST

A N American ranger threaded his way through willows bordering the banks of the St. Lawrence River. He kept asking Redcoats, "Has anybody seen the gen'ral?"

When the ranger arrived at a bay where soldiers worked to pull whaleboats to the bank, he waved his hand in a gesture passing for a salute and said to Jeffery Amherst, "Sir, Gen'ral, you hear the cannons? It was Fort Lévis. Blasted two advance guard row galleys out of the water and killed three rangers. One was from my home town in Massachusetts. We catched a Canadian woods-runner and loosened his tongue. He vows the fort's got thirty-seven cannon. Couldn't find the cap'n, so I thought I ought to come back and 'port in to you, sir."

August sunlight lancing through the hemlocks high-lighted the green jacket of the ranger and the gold-laced scarlet coat of the regal-looking general. Amherst's face, cold as a cemetery stone, gave no hint of his thoughts. He stroked his chin, wondering what to do.

Shafts of light made the forest look like a giant cathedral, except that it housed Amherst's army. In the woods along the river he had 10,960 armed men, half Redcoats, half colonials—including 706 wild Iroquois under Sir William Johnson. All save the Indians looked to Amherst for orders.

Amherst felt unsure of the Iroquois. When he had moved his army from Oswego to skirt Lake Ontario and float down the beautiful St. Lawrence, many of them had melted into the woods.

His target was Montreal. In closing on his goal, he would tighten an iron vise squeezing the French. Another British force was thrusting north toward Montreal up Lake Champlain and the Richelieu River. In addition, Murray, now a general, was leading Redcoats upstream from Quebec. His command had suffered in the city during the winter of 1759–1760 after Wolfe wrecked and captured it. Starvation and scurvy cut into Murray's army penned in the town by Canadians and French; about seven hundred Redcoats found graves outside the wall in the snow. Fortunately for Murray's men, a British fleet reappeared off Quebec in May, 1760.

Amherst's plan was for all three forces to converge at Montreal and defeat his enemy. Immediately, he had to decide what to do about Fort Lévis. This was bothersome.

The fort stood on a rocky, banjo-shaped, tiny island about one hundred miles upstream from Montreal (near present-day Ogdensburg, New York). Fort Lévis, 120 yards by 170, guarded the broad St. Lawrence at a point where it squeezed through a narrow race.

Amherst could portage the boats and bypass the fort, leaving it with a few men to watch it, but this was not General Amherst's way. Thomas Mante noted Amherst's thinking in his 1772 history of the war: "Making the garrison of the fort prisoners was alone a sufficient motive for attacking."

Amherst's plan was elaborate. His men in row-galleys attacked and, after a stiff fight, overwhelmed one of the two French warships guarding the fort. The other warship ran aground and was easily taken.

Amherst's idea for capturing the fort was to place riflemen in the tops of the gunboat *Onondaga,* firing down into the fort while grenadiers stormed the ramparts with broadswords and tomahawks. They would fill up the ditch around the fort with bundles of sticks (fascines) and climb over its ramparts with scaling ladders. But when the *Onondaga* crashed against a rocky ledge, the plan became unworkable. So the general ordered up the heavy 24-pounders and bombarded Lévis.

Buildings in the fort caught fire. Dirt ramparts, cradled by logs, sagged. The logs smoked and blazed. Fort Lévis looked like a frying pan on fire. Captain François Pouchot, the fort's commandant, ordered his drummers to beat a parley, and he ran up the red flag. The little fort, manned by three hundred men, was badly outnumbered, but taking it caused Amherst's army to pause for a week.

Iroquois screamed when the red flag went up, and prepared to tomahawk and scalp prisoners. General Amherst balked. Sir William warned that overcontrol would make the Indians quit. Amherst told Johnson that his army was sufficient without Indians, that he wanted their help but would not purchase it at the expense of barbarities.

When the Iroquois found they were restrained, many left in a rage. Some dug up the graves of French soldiers who had died defending the fort, and scalped the corpses. Johnson talked to the Indians before they departed, but with all his eloquence could hold on to only 170. Now, more than ever, Amherst had no use for Indians.

The general ordered the batteries of the fort leveled and damaged boats repaired, and proceeded down the St. Lawrence toward Montreal. When his flotilla ran through turbulent rapids, tragedy struck. Over sixty whaleboats capsized in the white water, eighty-four men drowned, and equipment and supplies were lost.

Amherst's plan for the three forces to converge on Montreal was uncoordinated, but it succeeded; the French were too weak to move against the various parts.

When Amherst hemmed in Governor de Vaudreuil's force, the Redcoat leader demanded the surrender, not just of Montreal, but of *all* Canada. Vaudreuil could do nothing but sign the capitulation and comply. The huge territory of Canada changed hands. The date was September 8, 1760.

The British and their colonials hoped for peace, but they were mistaken. Beneath the surface of daily affairs in eastern Canada, hatred, spawned by the war, continued to smolder. The French Canadians and the English were peoples of different cultures and religions. Feelings of distrust, favoritism, and rivalry between British and French would curse populations for many generations to come.

Shortly after Governor de Vaudreuil's surrender, a

Chippewa chief at Mackinac, in the Midwest, verbalized the attitude of many tribes. He said sharply to Alexander Henry, trader from New Jersey, "Englishman, you have conquered the French, but you have not yet conquered us."

Indians from the Midwest were even wilder than those in the east. Louis-Antoine de Bougainville, a French admiral who had served with Montcalm, wrote of western Indians:

> Canoe loads of Indians arrive every day. . . . No . . . interpreter understands their language. . . . They are naked save for a breechclout, and are painted black, red and blue, etc. Their heads are shaved and feathers ornament them. In their lengthened ear [lobes] are rings of brass wire. They have beaver skins for covering and carry lances, arrows, and quivers of buffalo skin. . . . Their dances seem like war dances of the Greeks.

They were not dancing around their campfires with joy. For years, the Indians had held the balance of power, with the French and British jockeying for their favor. The new way of the world upset the Indians far worse than any bitter wind that ever leveled trees and sank canoes on the lakes. The Indians could not adjust. French traders had showered them with presents. Now General Amherst, cold and distant, lashed out an order: "No more presents for Indians." He thought of this ancient custom as buying friendship. He also cut off guns and ammunition. Consequently, Indians were forced to hunt game again with bows and arrows. This meant less food.

However, it was the land and British forts on it that

rankled the Indians most. The British government's attitude toward the Indians' land was impossible for them
to understand. Britain recognized Indian ownership but
not their sovereignty and claimed the right of option to
buy. Also the British failed to oust all the squatters.
With the war over, Americans were streaming westward.
They wanted more land, and they had little consideration
for any Indians who happened to get in their way. The
British tried to stop them, but it was a hopeless task: There
were not enough soldiers to watch the whole frontier,
and the settlers slipped past them. When caught, they
simply waited for a better chance.

In addition, the haughty British attitude at conferences
upset the chiefs. They felt they were not given the dignity due them. To top it all, numbers of English traders
cheated and insulted the Indians.

French traders thought fast. They told the Indians that
the war was not over, and pointed at the fighting between
Britain and France still going on in Europe. "The King of
France is now awake," the traders said. "His soldiers will
come in greater numbers and run the Redcoats out."

Also the French made the Indians believe the British
would make them slaves. Thomas Mante observed, "No
people on the face of the earth are fuller of the idea of
liberty than the North American Indians."

The Briton who first found trouble cooking was the
white man who knew most about the Indians, Sir William
Johnson. Through his traders and contacts, he discovered
that the tribes were restless. Encouraged by General
Amherst, Johnson was not above stirring up intertribal
animosities as a means of keeping the Indians down.

Amherst wrote him: "[Have them] Fall upon One Another. . . ."

But when the Senecas of the Northwest showed signs of hostility, Johnson became alarmed and told the general that giving presents was cheaper than fighting a war. He sent a complaining note to Amherst: "Indian affairs are becoming harder. I wish I were clear of the management of them."

Amherst read this but looked on himself as a sort of supreme judge. After saying there would be no presents, he added, "I will use Indians as they deserve, reward them if they merit it, and punish them if they deserve it." He accepted reports of Indian discontent, but he was blind to its fury. And Amherst was handicapped: Most of his fine army had been ordered to service in the West Indies, and forts on the frontier held skeleton garrisons. Also the people in England had had their fill of war. It had fastened a debt of £140,000,000 on them, and in addition Pitt was out of office again.

With this involved situation as a foundation, the hour was nearing for an Indian uprising.

CHAPTER 21

PONTIAC TAKES THE WARPATH

OUT of the Ohio Valley rose a weird Indian. This was the Prophet, who traveled among the tribes spreading a religious message.

He talked as if he were on fire. "Indians must purify themselves," he shouted. The Prophet screamed that to be acceptable to the Great Spirit, Indians must turn away from the white man and go back to the primitive life of their forefathers. The Prophet wept and howled. Superstitious Indians traveled great distances in canoes and across country to hear him. But his idea of abandoning the white man's firearms caused his flame to sputter out.

A dynamic chief of the Ottawas, also a medicine man, seized part of the Prophet's message. The up-and-coming fifty-year-old Ottawa saw that all the tribes were now restless and might be united. He decided that survival of the Indian lay in joining together in a vast confederacy to defeat the might of the British Empire. He twisted the Prophet's message to "Love the French." This was Pontiac.

Forged letters from Frenchmen promising aid buoyed Chief Pontiac. When word was announced that the Treaty of Paris had been signed in early 1763, formally ending all fighting between France and Britain, Pontiac was even more certain he was right. The map of North America had been redrawn without the consent of a single Indian.

Pontiac went to work. He kept two secretaries, one a Frenchman, busy. With rare intelligence, this primitive leader organized the tribes to strike. He set May 2, 1763, as the day. Not only did Pontiac send messages, some written on birch bark, by his secretaries to chiefs over a wide area, but he traveled and talked to the tribes. His dynamic personality and uncommon oratory stirred them. Only four tribes remained neutral: the Sacs, Foxes, Winnebagos, and Menominees. With Pontiac and his tomahawk and war paint were Ottawas, Ojibwas, Potawatamis, Hurons, Miamis, Kickapoos, Wyandots, and Senecas.

Pontiac's uprising surprised the British. The frontiers of Pennsylvania, Maryland, and Virginia blazed in flames. White men were captured, tortured, and burned at the stake. A good many were boiled and eaten. Nine forts fell. Of the western ones, only Fort Pitt and Detroit remained. Pontiac and his remarkable conspiracy pushed the frontier eastward and gripped British and colonials with fear.

Pontiac chose for himself the destruction of Fort Detroit, the hardest fort to capture. He was schooled in war on a white man's standard; he was said to have taken part in Braddock's defeat and to have served on Lake

Claims were not firm

BRITISH

NEWFOUNDLAND

NEW SPAIN

Louisiana

TERRITORY
(Except New Orleans Area)

Atlantic

Ocean

Pacific Ocean

WEST INDIES

NORTH AMERICA AFTER TREATY OF PARIS
1763

France retained 2 islands off Newfoundland and part of West Indies

Map No. 4

Champlain under Montcalm, but he had to use Indian tactics. He had no artillery, but he was smart and brave.

Chief Pontiac's plan to take Detroit by trickery failed. Legend goes that the fort's commanding officer, Major Henry Gladwin, was warned of the plan by an Indian girl. Pontiac besieged the fort's garrison of 125 men with about nine hundred warriors, and decided to starve the British into surrender. In midsummer, the schooner *Michigan* sailed up the Detroit River to relieve the fort. Pontiac's Indians fired swarms of bullets into the vessel, but the sailors landed supplies and extended the life of the garrison.

General Amherst sent a relief expedition under Captain James Dalzel, who had 260 soldiers and the ace, Robert Rogers.

The rescue party arrived in little Fort Detroit under cover of night and fog. After two days of talking and worrying, Major Gladwin decided to send the soldiers and Rogers to strike Pontiac's camp.

The Indians were waiting a few miles from the palisade gate. They swept over Dalzel's force like a tidal wave. Dalzel went down, never to rise again. Rogers, with a handful of men, organized a rear guard and saved the soldiers from annihilation. A day later, the Indians cut out Dalzel's heart and rubbed it in the faces of the prisoners.

Pontiac's Indians were creating havoc over a wide area. In September, 1763, Senecas overpowered a wagon train and its guard of twenty-four soldiers near Niagara. The captives screamed as the Indians pushed them into the abyss of the Niagara River. It was obvious what the Indians were up to. Mr. John Stedman, in charge of the train, escaped being thrown in, and rode his horse through a hail of bullets to tell the tale.

Pontiac could lead Indians, but he could not change their nature. His warriors surrounding Detroit became restless. Siege warfare was not for them. Several of the tribes said they wanted peace. To the south, the Indians surrounding Fort Pitt worried because they discovered Amherst was sending an army under Colonel Bouquet. The Indians met and were decisively defeated by Bouquet in a hard battle near a stream called Bushy Run (twelve miles east of present-day Pittsburgh), and Fort Pitt was relieved.

By this time, Amherst was frantic because the war was dragging on and on. He ordered Bouquet to take no more prisoners and suggested to him a crude version of germ warfare: sending blankets infected with smallpox to the Indians.

At Detroit the siege continued, with Pontiac holding his Ottawas firm. When the valiant and stubborn chief received word that no help would come from the French, he realized he could not win. Pontiac's War now reached a stalemate.

In 1764, Colonel John Bradstreet advanced with an army into the Great Lakes region while Bouquet marched his soldiers farther into the Ohio country. The burly Bradstreet soon found himself trapped by British politics. He wanted to end the war, and being ambitious he also wanted to gain credit for making a satisfactory peace. He met with a council of Ottawas and Chippewas, listened to their side, and then granted them peace in an eight-paragraph document.

Bradstreet signed the treaty below the paragraph:

By the power and authority to me given and granted
by his Excellency the Honourable Major General
Thomas Gage, commander-in-chief of all his Majesty's
forces in North America.

The chiefs signed with their peculiar signatures: a Stork,
an Eel, and a Stag; a Deer with a Cross; a Turtle; an
Eagle with a Medal around its neck; and so on.

But when news of the peace treaty reached Gage, a
bombshell exploded. He reversed himself. General Gage
said he had never given Colonel Bradstreet any such power
even though Bradstreet carried appropriate orders signed
"Thomas Gage"!

Gage was jealous of Bradstreet, and the idea of the
colonel becoming important rankled him. In addition
to personal misgivings, apparently Gage had second
thoughts and now wanted Bradstreet and his men to act
in coordination with Colonel Bouquet and his army three
hundred miles to the south.

It is also possible that Sir William Johnson influenced
General Gage to reverse his orders. Johnson disliked
Bradstreet because that officer had spoiled several of Johnson's schemes to gain power and money. Bradstreet often
seemed to look for trouble, especially with his superiors,
and he had quarreled with many officers. It was a lesson:
no matter how efficient you are, you need to know how to
get along with your fellows.

A month after Bradstreet saw the chiefs draw their
peculiar signatures, Colonel Bouquet, a soldier of courage
but as ambitious as either Bradstreet or Johnson, addressed
the Indians near Fort Pitt: "You cover up your faults

[for the uprising] by blaming western Indians. . . . It is your duty to keep your young men in proper bounds and to chastise them if they do amiss."

Bouquet went on, upbraiding the Indians for their raids, for taking captives, and for murdering traders whom they had invited into the Fort Pitt area. He accused them of besieging Fort Pitt even though it was built with their permission. He demanded they surrender all prisoners to him—French as well as British.

The next day after Henry Bouquet's forceful speech, chiefs of the Delawares delivered eighteen captives to the fort with eighty-three small sticks, the number yet to come.

Indians who signed with Colonel Bradstreet kept the peace as a "sacred light," but those who treated with Colonel Bouquet were not as faithful. The frontier, especially around Fort Pitt, did not quiet down immediately.

But Pontiac's fight was over. He finally made a treaty in 1766 with Sir William Johnson and was pardoned. Five years later, this chief, who had tried to save Indian country from the white man, was murdered by another Indian.

In 1758, long before Pontiac and Johnson made their agreement, hatred put both white men and Cherokees on the warpath in South Carolina.

CHAPTER 22

CHEROKEE WAR PAINT

CHEROKEE CHIEF ATTAKULLACULLA was fifty-five years old and looked eighty. In 1758, the Redcoats in South Carolina called him "Little Carpenter" because when he worked to solve a political puzzle the pieces fell into place. He was an amazing Indian.

Of all the Cherokee chiefs, Attakullaculla looked the oddest. If the British had nicknamed him "Little Pincushion," they would have described his appearance well. He was slender and spindly-legged, with a little head sitting on pinched shoulders with no neck. A wrinkled brownish-red skin seemed to add to his age. He was small, but there was nothing tiny about his brain.

The chief's reputation for smartness and for being an effective diplomat commanded respect from both red and white men. Twenty-eight years before, with six other

Cherokees, Attakullaculla was transported to London to meet King George and other important people in London and to be entertained. The seven Indians were so impressed with their reception that they handed the British officials eagle feathers as symbols and said they looked on the King as their father. The Indians concluded, "In war, we will always be with you." This was in 1730.

Before that year, the Cherokees had given the British land in Cherokee country and permission to build forts. At the time this looked like a good idea to the Indians because the Redcoats explained the forts would protect them from the French. It was only fair in return, the Redcoats said, that in order to help the expense of building Fort Loudoun the Cherokees must fight Frenchmen. The English also gave the Cherokees arms so they could battle other Indians. The plans seemed wonderful.

Trouble flared up when the four hundred warriors left Ironhead Forbes in 1758 as he inched toward Fort Duquesne. The Cherokees made the six-hundred-mile trip back to South Carolina in small packs, some taking time out to steal horses and chickens and to set fire to settlers' cabins in Virginia.

This was not the first time the Cherokees had committed outrages in Virginia. Two years before, Virginians had slashed back at them because of horse and chicken raids, and twenty-four Cherokees had paid with their lives. Governor Dinwiddie, although he lived on a grand scale in his Williamsburg palace, descended to the level of the raiders by paying bounties for Cherokee scalps. After his trip to England, Chief Attakullaculla believed in the British. No Cherokee could criticize them in his presence. However, this fierce reaction of the Virginians

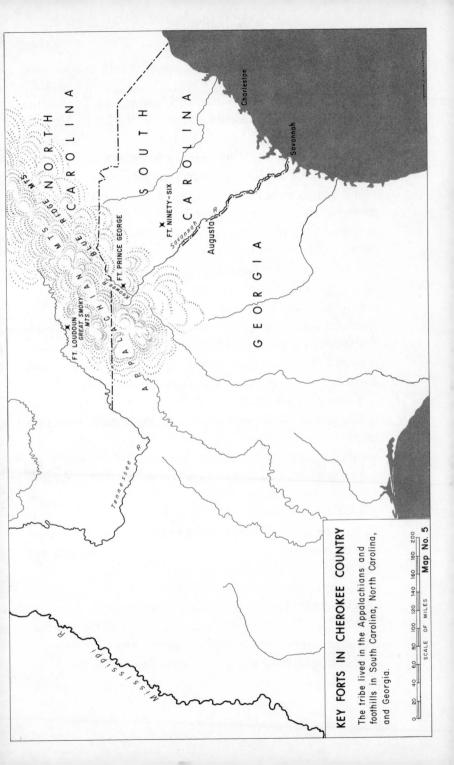

KEY FORTS IN CHEROKEE COUNTRY

The tribe lived in the Appalachians and foothills in South Carolina, North Carolina, and Georgia.

Map No. 5

SCALE OF MILES

0 20 40 60 80 100 120 140 160 180 200

in killing warriors upset him, and he mentally divided the white man's world, deciding that the British in Virginia were enemies.

A year after the Cherokees left Brigadier Forbes, a young Cherokee chief, Etowee, daubed on war paint. He could not rationalize the slaying of the twenty-four. To Etowee, all white men were enemies. It meant nothing to him or his warriors that word from the St. Lawrence River indicated that the British were winning the war.

Etowee and the Cherokees were angry over a number of things. Because of the war, not enough trade goods— weapons, ammunition, blankets, and other things they needed—were coming into Cherokee country. And traders who did come were cheats and seldom gave an Indian a square deal. In addition, some whites were stealing from them and on occasion killed Cherokees.

Etowee struck hard. He led his fighters in raids against lonely settlers in South Carolina, taking twenty-four lives as a mark of revenge. The number was becoming an evil symbol.

When South Carolina Governor William Henry Lyttelton, an odd-looking Britisher with a long nose and soulful eyes, heard of the slayings, he flew into a rage. Politicians in Charleston reflected his fury, and the bounty on scalps skyrocketed to £35 each. Thomas Mante noted the holocaust building up:

> Governor Lyttelton [was] convinced that it was only by an early and vigorous exertion of force that these Indians could be brought to reason. He determined to march against them as soon as possible.

[When he raised] 800 provincials and 300 regulars, he marched at their head into their country.

Lyttelton moved too fast, and citizens of South Carolina complained about his haste. The "army" he formed was ill prepared, miserable, and undisciplined. Nevertheless the governor was determined to bring the Indians to heel, so he summoned Cherokee chiefs to Charleston for a "peace conference." When they arrived, he was harsh. He wanted no talk. It was plain Governor Lyttelton was interested only in punishment for the Cherokees. The chiefs became prisoners. They could not leave town, and when Lyttelton placed himself at the head of his marching column, they trudged along as captives. The Indian leaders burned inwardly. Governor Lyttelton was not a wise man.

Riding ahead of his force was a messenger with word for Chief Attakullaculla to meet the governor at Fort Prince George. The Little Carpenter reported in buckskins, with a dirk the length of a bread knife at his belt. He had just returned at the head of a war party against the French, and exhibited scalps to prove it. The governor was not interested. As an anonymous writer of the times put it: "The Governor [had his thoughts] on the many Outrages . . . committed by the Cherokees on the Inhabitants of South Carolina."

Lyttelton harangued the Cherokee chiefs. He said if he made war on the Cherokees, their young men would be killed and their women carried into captivity. He insisted on a treaty. Its Article III was Mosaic "eye-for-an-eye" Law:

Whereas since the 19th of November, 1758, the Cherokees had slain divers of His Majesty's good Subjects . . . his Excellency demanding satisfaction . . . two Cherokee Indians of those guilty of the murders, having already been delivered up to be put to death, or otherwise disposed of as his Excellency the Governor shall direct; it is hereby agreed that twenty other Cherokee Indians, guilty of the murders, shall be delivered to the Governor to be put to death or otherwise disposed of.

Governor William Henry Lyttelton and six chiefs "set their hands and seals" to the treaty on December 26, 1759. Even though the awful number of hostages had slipped to twenty-two, the treaty was a perfect dish for Cherokee hotheads. Attakullaculla soon told the governor he could deliver only three hostages.

Regardless of the number turned over to the Redcoats, Cherokees took to the warpath. Back settlements were ravaged. Traders among the Indians, many of them unprincipled, became a special target and paid with their lives for their past unfairness.

The Cherokees swarmed against Fort Ninety-Six, so called because that was the number of miles the traders estimated it was from the town of Keowee, not far from the Blue Ridge. But Fort Ninety-Six was too strong for them. About the same time, the Indians surrounded lonely Fort Loudoun in the shadow of the Great Smokies. And Cherokees rushed torches into Orangeburg County, about eighty miles northwest of Charleston.

When the sad news of the attacks reached Governor William Bull, who followed Lyttelton in office, he sent a messenger to General Amherst, begging for help. The governor also readied an attack force.

In the meantime, a bitter drama occurred at Fort Prince George, a few miles north of present-day Clemson. The fort, near the headwaters of the Savannah River, was a reminder to the Cherokees of their disappointment in white men. The stronghold was ten log buildings surrounded by a palisade with bastion (spear-shaped) corners. That was all except for a shallow, dry moat circling the place. Inside the fort, soldiers, settlers, traders, and Indian hostages waited for the Cherokees to strike.

Cherokee Chief Oconostata, who was a bitter enemy of the British, planned the attack. He sauntered across the little bridge over the moat and rapped on the gate of the fort. When a sentry shouted a challenge, the chief said he wanted to speak to Lieutenant Richard Coytmore, the fort's commanding officer. This was death calling Coytmore.

Three men came out: Coytmore, Ensign Bell, and Mr. Doharty (probably "Dougherty"), who was an interpreter. The chief lured them to the riverbank. Suddenly, the Cherokee whirled a bridle he carried in his hand. At this signal, a volley crashed out of a nearby thicket. Down went all three Englishmen. Redcoats tore out of the fort to the rescue, as cannons belched grapeshot at the Indians. But all the Redcoats could do was to carry the dying lieutenant and his two wounded companions into the fort. The Indians left in a hurry.

Ensign Milne, now the leader in the fort, ordered the Indian hostages placed in irons and confined to the guardhouse. But the hostages broke out a tomahawk that had been smuggled in by a friend, killing one Redcoat and wounding another. This brought the garrison to the verge of panic. In a twinkling, the hostages were slain.

The Cherokees attacked the fort, but failed to take it.

Finally, in early April, 1760, help arrived for the Redcoats when six transports sailed into Charleston Harbor. On board were thirteen hundred men and officers, including rugged Highlanders sent by Amherst, to march against the Cherokees. Colonel Archibald Montgomery was in command, but he worked under a handicap because General Amherst had told him before he sailed for Carolina, "I want these soldiers back for a campaign in Canada."

News of the arrival of the Redcoats sped through the Cherokee grapevine, but the Indians did not scare easily. Some had witnessed Braddock's defeat, others still laughed at Forbes's idea of building a string of forts in the forest leading to Fort Duquesne. The Cherokees believed they could win over any Redcoats who ever lived.

Colonel Montgomery lashed out into Cherokee country. That spring, George Washington had written an estimation of Montgomery's enemy: ". . . crafty, subtle [warriors] that gave trouble when least expected."

Montgomery believed in the torch, and he put on a show more vicious than any the Cherokees had ever staged. He said the only way to win was to destroy Cherokee food supplies. On his way to relieve beleaguered Fort Loudoun, Montgomery burned five Indian villages and adjacent cornfields and gardens. He killed well over sixty Indians. He could not, however, get far into the mountains because he lacked supply trains, and there were no forts to give him supplies.

In a red-hot fire of revenge, the Cherokees went after

the Redcoats, ambushing them in a narrow valley and wounding Colonel Montgomery. The Cherokees had to withdraw, but their morale was high. The Redcoats' raid had united them as never before. They were determined to win. They were helped by smallpox. The dread disease had scourged them many times. When the pestilence attacked the Redcoats, Montgomery suddenly remembered that Amherst wanted his men back.

So Montgomery put his soldiers on the road to Charleston, where he announced that he was "taking shipping for New York." He did leave four hundred Royal Scots behind in Charleston, but they were four hundred miles over bad roads from surrounded Fort Loudoun. His campaign had not been a success, although he left the Cherokees badly weakened.

The choice of the one hundred Redcoats and the one hundred colonial soldiers penned in Fort Loudoun was terrible: surrender to the Indians or starve. For six months the Loudoun garrison had existed on vegetables it could grow, and on horsemeat. Occasionally, brave men slipped out of the stockade at night to barter clothing (literally off their backs) with Indian women for corn. Clothes also bought four steers. But in June, 1760, the chiefs shut off all supplies. Chief Attakullaculla, the Little Carpenter, worked for peace until Cherokees from nearby hills told him to leave or be killed.

Fort Loudoun's commanding officer, Captain Raymond Demere, asked his officers in August to decide what was best. In a letter to him that ended "SIGNED BY ALL THE OFFICERS," the leaders agreed their only course lay in asking Captain John Stuart to treat with the Indians for the best terms possible.

Stuart, a smart, pleasant Scot, loved by the Indians, got them to agree to let the garrison surrender and march away. The soldiers had to give the delighted Cherokees most of their ammunition. Captain Demere performed the hard job of hauling down the Union Jack. Out marched the soldiers, through crowds of howling Indians.

Accounts as to what happened disagree. It appears that at the end of fifteen miles the Indians said it was their turn to take hostages. They wanted the same number the white man had taken, but they miscounted. They seized three officers and twenty-three privates and killed them. Captain Demere was scalped and made to dance. After he fell dead, the rest of the garrison were distributed among the tribe as slaves. The Indians spared Captain Stuart, telling him he could go free if he would show them how to fire the cannons they were taking from the fort. Stuart was excused from this, as Little Carpenter appeared and spirited him away under the pretext of taking him hunting.

In the spring, the Cherokees decided it was time to end the war. Because of Montgomery's destruction of their crops, many were hungry and dispirited. The governments of Virginia, North Carolina, and South Carolina were readying themselves (or trying to) to strike Indians in a white man's revenge. The Cherokees' "We will bury the hatchet" went unnoticed.

General Amherst sent two thousand Redcoats to Charleston under Colonel James Grant, who had served with Montgomery. Soon, fifteen Cherokee towns went up in smoke and flames. The Cherokees fled to the swamps. Chief Attakullaculla asked for peace and was refused. Fire, starvation, and fighting forced the Cherokees to their knees. Carolinians who would become famous in the American Revolution helped suppress the Indians: Henry Laurens, John and William Moultrie, Francis Marion, Isaac Huger, and Andrew Pickens.

Colonel Grant hated the war and said the Carolinians were mostly to blame. Finally Governor Bull sent for Little Carpenter, and they smoked an overdue pipe of peace. A few of the captive soldiers had been tortured to death, but most of them now were ransomed or released. The war with the Cherokees was over. It ruined the Indians and proved costly to the colonists.

In the early fall of 1761, two years after Quebec fell, Attakullaculla and Governor Bull signed a treaty. Stuart, at the request of the Indians, became "chief white man" Indian agent to represent them and to care for them.

In 1763, King George III issued a royal proclamation. It "closed to our loving subjects" purchase of land as well as the right to settle in the huge region between the Alleghenies and the Mississippi, from Florida to Quebec. Nevertheless, in five years about thirty thousand white settlers crossed the mountains into Indian land, a vanguard of more to come.

The plight of the Wappingers is characteristic of the white man's treatment of the red man. The Wappingers, a loose confederacy of Indians living along the Hudson River, on the New York–Connecticut border and on Long Island, left home at various times to help fight Britain's battles. But no Indians, not even the Stockbridge Indians who fought so loyally under Robert Rogers, went to war for more than a few months at a time. During the years the Wappinger warriors helped Britain, white men occupied more and more of their territory. By the end of the French and Indian War, white settlers had appropriated 204,800 acres of Wappinger land.

The Indians complained and in court tried without success to understand the language of lawyers. King George III, to his credit, became exercised over the injustice to his Indian subjects and used his influence to try to right the wrong. But there was little he could do. The Council of New York acted, deciding against the Indians because they had never registered legal title to the land.

The future of Indians in North America was clinched by the French and Indian War, a war that gained for Britain most of the continent.

APPENDIX I

*Résumé of the Four Colonial Wars That Preceded
the French and Indian War of 1754–1763,
and Allied Wars in Europe*

The four colonial wars preceding the French and Indian
War were extensions in subordinate relationship to wars on
the continent of Europe. The conflicts are listed below in
two columns.

Old World Phase	New World Phase
War of the Grand Alliance, sometimes called the War of the League of Augsburg. Pitted against France from 1689 to 1697 were England, Holland, the Holy Roman Empire, and other allies. Louis XIV of France was stopped in his effort to acquire complete military dominance of Europe. The war ended in a stalemate with Louis's finances exhausted.	*King William's War* (1689–1697) started between the English and French at Hudson Bay and along the St. Lawrence and Mohawk Rivers over fishing areas and the fur trade. The French also warred with the Iroquois.
The Treaty of Ryswick failed to solve problems of Europe.	The Massachusetts Bay Colony decided Canada must be destroyed because of bloody French and Indian raids on Schenectady, New York, Salmon Falls, New Hampshire, and Falmouth, Maine (near modern Portland). Consequently, Sir William Phips captured Port Royal, Canada (near Annapolis Royal, Nova Scotia), with a small naval force, in 1690. Phips next tried to, but could not, take Quebec; his force was too undis-

ciplined to overcome the French under Frontenac.

The Treaty of Ryswick practically invited further war, and indeed after it was signed in 1697 soldiers of New England fought engagements against Indians for two years.

War of the Spanish Succession was the second round in a series of wars raging from 1701 to 1713. By this war, England and her allies, the Netherlands, Austria, Prussia, and others, sought to prevent a close union of France and Spain, which would have upset both the European balance of power and established trade relations.

The war was almost a disaster for France. However, France signed a separate peace, the Treaty of Utrecht, in 1713 with Great Britain and the Netherlands, which, among other provisions, confirmed the Bourbon Philip V, friendly to France, as King of Spain. It was a futile war. However, England's capture of Gibraltar aided the British Empire for over two centuries.

Queen Anne's War began in 1702 with a conflict in America's southern frontier. Spain was an ally of France. South Carolina struck against the Spanish at St. Augustine, Florida.

However, the main theater of war was New England. French and Indians raided Deerfield, Massachusetts, and other settlements in Maine (then part of Massachusetts) were destroyed for the second time. Colonel Benjamin Church led New Englanders to seize Port Royal and destroy Indian and Canadian villages in Acadia, now Nova Scotia, while French and Indians captured villages on the eastern shore of Newfoundland.

British colonists were disappointed that aid from England was delayed, and further, when it did arrive in 1711, eight vessels with about 1,000 men were lost in the St. Lawrence River.

Fighting raged in the West Indies.

The weak Treaty of Utrecht failed to stop border warfare that ran on for nearly a year, and failed to define the boundaries of Acadia and the Hudson Bay area. Further conflict sprang from this ineffective treaty. From Louis XIV's point of view the treaty was especially bad. Newfoundland, the Hudson Bay area, and all of Acadia, except Cape Breton and Île St. Jean (Prince Edward Island) were ceded to England.

War of Jenkins' Ear started in 1739. It sprang from a provision in the Treaty of Utrecht that let England send one ship each year to Spain's overseas ports, otherwise closed to all non-Spanish ships. England used this to smuggle cargo, and Spain reacted by searching English ships. When Spaniards seized the ship of Robert Jenkins and cut off one of his ears, Great Britain declared war on Spain. Consequently, a British fleet sailed into the Caribbean to punish Spaniards. Though reinforced by 4,000 American volunteers, this expedition was a costly failure.

"War in the South" broke out when Georgia was founded as a British colony. General James Oglethorpe, Georgia's governor, tried to give poor debtors a new start in America. Britain was interested; it would mean another colony.

Spain started the fighting by capturing a fort built by Oglethorpe at the mouth of the St. Marys River. Oglethorpe struck back with a mixed force of regulars, rangers, Highlanders, and Chickasaw and Cherokee Indians. Fighting spread through the Caribbean.

The war ended in 1748, but again disputed boundaries were not fixed—this time in the south.

War of the Austrian Succession, from 1740 to 1748, was a series of European conflicts, the principal struggle being between Prussia and Austria over Silesia. England, Holland, Austria, and Saxony allied themselves against

King George's War, of 1744 to 1748, was not prosecuted vigorously in America, although William Pepperrell, with the help of a British fleet, led New Englanders to capture the French fortress of Louisbourg.

France, Spain, Prussia, and Bavaria. It was a general war fought in the Netherlands, the Rhineland, Bohemia, and Italy. Maurice de Saxe, the outstanding Marshal of France, one of the best generals of the age, repeatedly defeated the English, Austrians, and the Dutch. Peace came with the Treaty of Aix-la-Chapelle.

French and Indians raided towns along the northern frontier; while Sir William Johnson launched Mohawk attacks against the French. In retaliation, the French and Indians burned Saratoga, New York.

The weak peace treaty of 1748 (Aix-la-Chapelle) did little except restore the status that existed before the war and returned the Louisbourg fortress to France, to the disgust of New Englanders.

The foregoing wars failed to solve the question: Who was to rule in North America—England, France, or Spain? The French and Indian War of 1754–1763, which was paralleled in Europe by the Seven Years' War of 1756–1763, would settle it.

After two years of fighting, which began with brawls between French and English fur traders and grew into battles between their regular troops, England declared war on France on May 18, 1756.

APPENDIX II

Explanation of the Term "Brigadier"

This is an unusual rank and title, not employed in the United States Army.

In the British Army, "brigadier" is an appointment for an officer—usually an experienced lieutenant colonel or colonel—to the command of a corps consisting of several battalions, called a brigade.

It is a wartime title. At the end of the war, the brigadier reverts to the rank and title he held when he received the initial orders.

Brigadiers have authority equal to that of a brigadier general in the United States Army, and as a courtesy are called "general." However, it would be incorrect to refer in writing to Brigadier Smith as Brigadier General Smith.

FURTHER READING

I referred to many books. My principal sources follow:

Adams, Charles Francis, *Massachusetts, Its Historians and Its History*. Boston, Houghton Mifflin & Co., 1893.

Alberts, Robert C., *The Fantastic Adventures of Captain Stobo*. New York, American Heritage Publishing Co., 1963.

Amherst, Jeffery, *The Journal of Jeffery Amherst, 1758 to 1763*. Toronto, The Ryerson Press, 1931.

Bougainville, Louis Antoine de, *Adventure in the Wilderness; the American Journals of Louis Antoine de Bougainville, 1756–1760*, Edward P. Hamilton, trans. and ed. Norman, Okla., University of Oklahoma Press, 1964. (Fascinating; describes French dealings with the Indians.)

Brownell, Charles DeWolf, *The Indian Races of North and South America*. New York, H. E. and S. S. Scranton, 1853.

Buell, Augustus C., *Sir William Johnson*. New York, D. Appleton & Co., 1903. (Not outstanding, except for excellent description of Johnson. Contains some inaccuracies.)

The Capital Region. Albany, N.Y., brochure, New York World's Fair, 1939.

Chamberlain, Samuel, *Frontier of Freedom*. New York, Hastings House, 1957. (Helpful re: Deerfield Raid of 1704.)

———— *Six New England Villages*. New York, Hastings House, 1948. (Helpful re: Deerfield Raid of 1704.)

Chidsey, Donald Barr, *The French and Indian War*. New York, Crown Publishers, Inc., 1969.

Churchill, Winston S., *A History of the English-Speaking Peoples; The Age of Revolution.* New York, Dodd, Mead and Co., 1957. (Contains broad outline of the war.)

Clarke, Thomas Wood, *The Bloody Mohawk.* New York, The Macmillan Co., 1940.

Corkran, David H., *The Cherokee Frontier; Conflict and Survival, 1740–62.* Norman, Okla., University of Oklahoma Press, 1962.

Cuneo, John R., *Robert Rogers of the Rangers.* New York, Oxford University Press, 1959. (The best account of the famous ranger.)

Darlington, Mary Cason, *History of Colonel Henry Bouquet.* Printed privately, 1920.

DeVoto, Bernard, *The Course of Empire.* Boston, Houghton Mifflin Co., 1952. (Excellent broad but brief picture of the era.)

Diefendorf, Mary Riggs, *The Historic Mohawk.* New York, G. P. Putnam's Sons, 1910.

Downey, Fairfax, *Louisbourg: Key to a Continent.* Englewood Cliffs, N.J., Prentice-Hall, Inc., 1965. (Careful descriptions.)

Drake, Samuel Adams, *The Border Wars of New England.* New York, Charles Scribner's Sons, 1897.

Driver, Harold Edson, *Indians of North America.* Chicago, University of Chicago Press, 1961. (Thorough examination of Indian life.)

Eccles, William John, *Frontenac, the Courtier Governor.* Toronto, McClelland & Stewart, Ltd., 1959.

Fairchild, Byron, *Messrs. William Pepperrell: Merchants at Piscataqua.* Ithaca, N.Y., Cornell University Press, 1954.

Federal Writers' Project, "Albany—Past and Present," in *New York: Guide to the Empire State,* "American Guide Series." New York, Oxford University Press, 1940.

Fernow, Berthold, *The Ohio Valley in Colonial Days.* Albany, N.Y., J. Munsell's Sons, 1890.

Fisher, Sydney George, *The True Benjamin Franklin.* Philadelphia, J. B. Lippincott Co., 1899.

Flexner, James Thomas, *Mohawk Baronet*. New York, Harper & Brothers, 1959. (Superior picture of Johnson, his life and times.)

Franklin, Benjamin, *Autobiography of Benjamin Franklin*, Leonard W. Labaree, Ralph L. Ketcham, Helen C. Boatfield, and Helene H. Fineman, eds. New Haven, Conn., Yale University Press, 1964.

Freeman, Douglas Southall, *George Washington, a Biography*, vols. 1 and 2. New York, Charles Scribner's Sons, 1948–1957. (Excellent detail.)

Furnas, J. C., *The Americans; A Social History of the United States, 1587–1914*. New York, G. P. Putnam's Sons, 1969.

Glenn, James, and Milligen-Johnston, George, *Colonial South Carolina*, Chapman J. Milling, ed. Columbia, S.C., University of South Carolina Press, 1951. (Interesting historical documents and accounts.)

Green, Walford Davis, *William Pitt*. New York, G. P. Putnam's Sons, 1901.

Greene, Nelson, *The Valley of the Hudson; River of Destiny*, vol. 1. Chicago, The S. J. Clarke Publishing Co., 1931.

Griffis, William Elliott, *Sir William Johnson and the Six Nations*. New York, Dodd, Mead and Co., 1891.

Hale, Edward Everett, *The Story of Massachusetts*. Boston, D. Lothrop & Co., 1891. (Helpful re: Deerfield Raid and early Louisbourg.)

Hamilton, Edward P., *The French and Indian Wars*. New York, Doubleday & Co., Inc., 1962. (Excellent account.)

Hart, Gerald E., *The Fall of New France, 1755–1760*. New York, G. P. Putnam's Sons, 1888.

Hulbert, Archer Butler, *Washington's Road, the First Chapter of the Old French War*. Cleveland, The A. H. Clark Co., 1903.

Hunt, George T., *Wars of the Iroquois, a Study in Intertribal Relations*. Madison, The University of Wisconsin Press, 1940. (Scholarly treatise.)

Jackson, Harold McGill, *Rogers' Rangers*. Ottawa, 1953.

James, Alfred Procter, and Stotz, Charles Morse, *Drums in the Forest*. Pittsburgh, The Historical Society of Western Pennsylvania, 1958. (Best available descriptions of various frontier forts.)

Johnson, William, *The Papers of Sir William Johnson*, vols. 1 and 13. Albany, N.Y., The University of the State of New York, 1921.

Josephy, Alvin M., Jr., ed., *The American Heritage Book of Indians*. New York, American Publishing Co., 1961.

Journals of Major Robert Rogers. New York, Corinth Books, 1961.

Kenton, Edna, ed., *Black Gown and Redskins*. London & New York, Longmans, Green & Co., 1956.

Lanctot, Gustave, *A History of Canada*, trans. by Margaret M. Cameron. Cambridge, Mass., Harvard University Press, 1965.

Livingston, William, *A Review of the Military Operations in North America . . . with observations, characters, and anecdotes*. Dublin, P. Wilson and J. Exchaw, 1757.

Lloyd, Christopher, *The Capture of Quebec*. New York, The Macmillan Co., 1959. (Delightful.)

Loescher, Burt Garfield, *Rogers' Rangers*. San Mateo, Calif., n.p., 1969. (Not entirely accurate.)

Long, John Cuthbert, *Lord Jeffery Amherst*. New York, The Macmillan Co., 1933.

McCardell, Lee, *Ill-Starred General: Braddock of the Coldstream Guards*. Pittsburgh, University of Pittsburgh Press, 1958. (Probably the best on Braddock.)

McCormac, Eugene Irving, *Colonial Opposition to Imperial Authority During the French and Indian War*. Berkeley, Calif., The University Press, 1911.

McCracken, Henry Noble, *Old Dutchess Forever!* New York, Hastings House, 1956. (History of a New York county.)

McCrady, Edward, *The History of South Carolina Under the Royal Government, 1719–1776*. London: MacMillan & Co., Ltd., 1899.

McLennan, John Stewart, *Louisbourg*. Sydney, N.S., Fortress Press, 1957.

Macleod, William Christie, *The American Indian Frontier*. New York, Alfred A. Knopf, 1928.

Mante, Thomas, *The History of the Late War in North America, and the Islands in the West Indies, including the campaigns of MDCCLXIII and MDCCLXIV against His Majesty's Indian Enemies*. London. Printed for W. Strahan and T. Cadell, 1772. (Mante served in the war. His book carries a flavor and gives a wide vista.)

Mayo, Lawrence Shaw, *Jeffery Amherst*. New York, Longmans, Green & Co., 1916.

Miller, William, *A New History of the United States*. New York, George Braziller, Inc., 1958. (Excellent account of pre-French and Indian War conditions.)

Morris, Richard B., *Encyclopedia of American History*. New York, Harper & Brothers, 1953.

Nolan, James B., *General Benjamin Franklin*. Philadelphia, University of Pennsylvania Press, 1936.

Pargellis, Stanley McCrory, *Lord Loudoun in North America*. New Haven, Conn., Yale University Press, 1933. (Outstanding presentation of logistical and administrative problems facing the British.)

Parkman, Francis, *The Conspiracy of Pontiac and the Indian War*, Vols. 10 and 11. Boston, Little, Brown & Co., 1874.

——— *The Seven Years' War (Narrative Taken from Montcalm and Wolfe, The Conspiracy of Pontiac, and a Half-Century of Conflict)*, John H. McCallum, ed. New York, Harper Torchbooks, 1968. (Parkman has long been considered the best secondary source and is still invaluable, though Hamilton may have replaced him. Parkman's major weakness is his lack of understanding of the military forces involved.)

Peck, Anne Merriman, *The Pageant of Canadian History*. New York, Longmans, Green & Co., 1943. (Excellent view from Canada.)

Peckham, Howard H., *The Colonial Wars, 1689–1762*. Chicago, The University of Chicago Press, 1964. (Superior summary and outline.)

Peterson, Harold L., *Arms and Armor in Colonial America*. New York, Bramhall House, 1956. (The authoritative work on this subject.)

Pouchot, Monsieur, *Memoir upon the Late War in North America between the French and English, 1755–1760*. Roxbury, Mass., printed for W. Elliot Woodward, 1866.

Putnam, Rufus, *Journal of Gen. Rufus Putnam kept in northern New York during four campaigns of the old French and Indian War, 1757–1760*. Albany, N.Y., J. Munsell's Sons, 1886.

Reid, William Max, *Old Fort Johnson*. New York, G. P. Putnam's Sons, 1906.

Roberts, Kenneth, *Northwest Passage*. New York, Doubleday & Co., Inc., 1937. (Exciting historical fiction about Rogers' most famous raid.)

Rogers, Robert, *Journals of Major Robert Rogers*, New York, Corinth Books, Inc., 1961.

Schutz, John A., *William Shirley, Governor of Massachusetts*. Chapel Hill, N.C., University of North Carolina Press, 1961.

Shirley, William, *Correspondence of William Shirley, governor of Massachusetts and military commander in America, 1731–1760*, 2 vols., Charles Henry Lincoln, ed. New York, The Macmillan Co., 1912.

Stacey, Charles Perry, *Quebec, 1759*. Toronto, The Macmillan Co., 1959. (Factual and interesting.)

Stanley, George Francis Gilman, *Canada's Soldiers*. Toronto, The Macmillan Co. of Canada, 1960.

——— *New France: The Last Phase, 1744–1760*. Toronto, McClelland & Stewart, Ltd., 1968. (Illuminates Canadian history of the war.)

Steele, Matthew Forney, *American Campaigns*, 2 vols. Washington, D.C., Byron S. Adams, 1909. (Excellent outline, including text and maps.)

Stobo, Robert, *Memoirs of Major Robert Stobo of the Virginia Regiment*. Pittsburgh, J. S. Davidson, 1854.

Stone, William Leete, *The Life and Times of Sir William Johnson, Bart*, 2 vols., Albany, N.Y., J. Munsell, 1865.

Thomson, Charles, *Causes of the Alienation of the Delaware and Shawanese Indians from the British Interest*. Philadelphia, John Campbell, 1867.

Thwaites, Reuben Gold, ed., *The Jesuit Relations and Allied Documents*, Vol. 31. Cleveland, The Burrows Brothers Co., 1896–1901. (Re: Indians.)

Tunstall, Brian William Cuthbert, *William Pitt, Earl of Chatham*. London, Hodder & Stoughton Ltd., 1938.

Van Every, Dale, *Forth to the Wilderness, The First American Frontier, 1754–1774*. New York, William Morrow & Co., 1961.

Volwiler, Albert T., *George Croghan and the Westward Movement, 1741–1782*. Cleveland, The Arthur H. Clark Co., 1926.

Washington, George, *The Writings of George Washington from the Original Manuscript Sources, 1745–1799*, vol. 1., John C. Fitzpatrick, ed. Washington, D.C., United States Government Printing Office, 1931.

Weise, Arthur James, *History of the City of Albany*. Albany, N.Y., E. H. Bender, 1884.

The West Point Atlas of American Wars, Vincent J. Esposito, ed. New York, Frederick A. Praeger, 1964. (Maps illustrating the war and outline.)

Williams, John, *The Redeemed Captive Returning to Zion*, reprint of 6th ed. Ann Arbor, Mich., University Microfilms, Inc., 1966. (The original and best account of the Deerfield Raid.)

Wood, Norman Barton, *Lives of Famous Indian Chiefs*. Aurora, Ill., American Indian Historical Publishing Co., 1906.

Woodward, Grace Steele, *The Cherokees*. Norman, Okla., University of Oklahoma Press, 1963. (Instructive.)

Wrexall, Peter, *An Abridgment of the Indian Affairs*. Cambridge, Mass., Harvard University Press, 1915. (Important historical document, written in 1754. Its "Introduction" by Charles Howard McIlwain gives superior summary of role of the Iroquois.)

Wrong, George M., *The Conquest of New France*. New Haven, Conn., Yale University Press, 1918. (Skeletal but valuable picture of conditions and the war.)

INDEX